HAPPINESS

HAPPINESS
A PHILOSOPHER'S GUIDE

FRÉDÉRIC LENOIR

Translated by Andrew Brown

MELVILLE HOUSE
BROOKLYN · LONDON

HAPPINESS: A PHILOSOPHER'S JOURNEY

First published in France as *Du bonheur: Un voyage philosophique*
Copyright © 2013 by Librairie Arthème Fayard
Translation copyright © 2015 by Andrew Brown

First Melville House printing: April 2015

Melville House Publishing   8 Blackstock Mews
    145 Plymouth Street   and Islington
    Brooklyn, NY 11201   London N4 2BT

mhpbooks.com   facebook.com/mhpbooks   @melvillehouse

Library of Congress Cataloging-in-Publication Data
Lenoir, Frédéric.
    [Du bonheur. English]
    Happiness : a philosopher's guide / Frédéric Lenoir ;
translated by Andrew Brown. — 1st ed.
        pages   cm
    Includes bibliographical references.
    ISBN 978-1-61219-439-4 (hardcover)
    ISBN 978-1-61219-441-7 (ebook)
    1. Happiness. I. Title.

B187.H3L4613 2015
152.4'2—dc23

                              2014040205

Design by Christopher King

Printed in the United States of America
    1 3 5 7 9 10 8 6 4 2

CONTENTS

HAPPINESS

Prologue

So we must exercise ourselves in the things which
bring happiness, since, if that be present, we have
everything, and, if that be absent, all our actions are
directed towards attaining it.[1]

—Epicurus

For many years, I've been planning to write a book about
happiness. And for many years, I've kept putting it off.
Although the quest for happiness is probably the most
widely shared thing in the world, it isn't easy to write
about it. Like many people, I'm irritated by the way the
word is used here, there and everywhere, especially in
advertising, and by the flood of books that claim to provide "recipes" for happiness. The question of happiness
is forever being discussed: eventually it gets worn down
and loses its edge. But although it's become so common-
place, and seems so simple, it's still an enthralling question, one that involves a whole skein of factors not easy
to untangle.

This stems from the very nature of happiness: In some
ways, it can't be grasped, any more than wind or water.
No sooner do you think you've got hold of it than it slips

through your fingers. If you try to nail it down, it evades you. Sometimes it escapes just when you think you're onto it, and suddenly it pops up when you're least expecting it. And sometimes you only recognize it after some mishap has befallen you. "I recognized happiness from the noise it made as it left," as Jacques Prévert elegantly put it. However, as I've discovered from my own experience, the pursuit of happiness isn't a pointless quest. We really *can* be happier if we think about our lives, if we work on ourselves, if we learn to make more sensible decisions, or indeed if we alter our thoughts, our beliefs, or the way we imagine ourselves and the world. The great paradox of happiness is that it can be tamed while still remaining essentially beyond our control. Happiness is a matter of fate and chance; but it can also stem from a rational, deliberate approach. Nearly twenty-five centuries ago, the Greek philosopher Aristotle was already emphasizing its ambiguity: "For this reason also the question is asked, whether happiness is to be acquired by learning or by habituation or some other sort of training, or comes in virtue of some divine providence or again by chance."[2]

Another difficulty arises from the notably *relative* character of happiness: it varies with each culture and each individual, and, in every person, from one phase of life to the next. It often takes on the guise of things we don't have: for someone who is ill, happiness lies in health; for someone who is unemployed, it's in work; for some single people, it lies in being a couple—and, for some married people, in being single again! These disparities are heightened by a subjective dimension: artists are happy when practicing their art, intellectuals when handling concepts, romantics when they are in love. Sigmund

Freud, the father of psychoanalysis, shed considerable light on this point when he noted:

> In this, [the individual's] psychical constitution will play a decisive part, irrespectively of the external circumstances. The man who is predominantly erotic will give first preference to his emotional relationships with other people; the narcissistic man, who inclines to be more self-sufficient, will seek his main satisfactions in his internal mental processes; the man of action will never give up on the external world on which he can try out his strength.[3]

This is one of the reasons why there is no "recipe" for happiness that would work for everybody.

So is all philosophical reflection on happiness futile? In my view, not at all. However interesting it may be to emphasize and understand the elusive, relative and subjective character of happiness, this is not the end of the story. The laws of life and the way human beings function also have a major impact on happiness, and these can be grasped both through traditional philosophical reflection and through several scientific approaches: psychology, sociology, biology and the cognitive sciences. And if, in the twenty-first century, philosophers have anything new to tell us about the subject that hasn't already been said by the thinkers of the past, this will probably be the result of their drawing on the findings of contemporary science. They will also benefit from bringing together different types of knowledge (even the most ancient), since these days, fortunately, we have access to the thoughts of the sages of all the great cultures of the world. Pythagoras, the Buddha and Confucius would have been able to hold a dialogue with each other, as they were probably contemporaries—but geographical and linguistic barriers would have rendered any such encounter highly unlikely. However, in our day, such an encounter can indeed take place, as we can compare and contrast those of their texts that have been handed down to posterity. And we can make the most of this opportunity.

Because the ancients were convinced of the random and, in the final analysis, fundamentally unjust character of happiness, the various etymologies of the word almost always invoke a notion of luck or favorable destiny. In Greek, the word for happiness, *eudaimonia,* can be taken to mean "having a good *daimon.*" These days, we would say "having a guardian angel," or "being born under a lucky star." In French, *bonheur* comes from the Latin *bonum augurium*: "good omen" or "good fortune." In English, *happiness* comes from the Icelandic root *happ*, "luck" or "chance," and there is indeed a large element of "luck" in being happy, if only because happiness is, as we shall see, to a large degree based on our sensibility, on our biological inheritance, on the family and social environment in which we were born and grew up, on the surroundings in which we develop and on the encounters that mark our lives.

If this is so, if we are inclined by our nature or fate to be happy or unhappy, can thinking about happiness help us to be any happier? I believe so. Experience, supported by several scientific studies, shows that we also bear a certain responsibility for being (or not being) happy. Happiness is out of our control and yet depends on us.

We are *conditioned* but not *determined* by various factors to be more or less happy. So, by using our reason and will, for example, we have the ability to increase our capacity for happiness (though the success of our quest is not thereby guaranteed). Because they shared this conviction, many philosophers have written books purportedly on "ethics," devoted to what will encourage us to lead the best and happiest lives imaginable. And isn't this philosophy's main rationale? Epicurus, a sage from Athens who lived shortly after Aristotle, points out that "in the study of philosophy, pleasure accompanies growing knowledge; for pleasure does not follow learning; rather, learning and pleasure advance side by side."⁴ This quest for a "good" or "happy" life is called *wisdom*. That is why, etymologically, the word *philosophy* means "love of wisdom." Philosophy teaches us to think well so as to try and live better. But, in this area, philosophy is not just a matter of thinking: it also has a practical side and can, as for the ancients, take the form of psychological and spiritual exercises. The modern university trains specialists; ancient philosophy was out to shape human beings. As Pierre Hadot has showed throughout his work, "philosophy in antiquity was a spiritual exercise."⁵ Most works by Greek and Roman philosophers "were the products of a philosophical school, in the most concrete sense of the term, in which a master forms his disciples, trying to guide them to self-transformation and -realization."⁶

So it is a philosophical journey, in this broader sense, that I would like to propose to the reader. There is nothing linear about the route, which won't be following the chronological order of the authors' lives or the emergence of concepts: this would be conventional and boring. It is, instead, a ramble, the most exciting imaginable, with many questions and concrete examples on the way. On this journey, the reader will encounter the analyses of various psychologists as well as science's latest contributions. It is, above all, a journey in which, through questions and answers, drawing on various rules for living and spiritual exercises, the reader will be walking alongside those giants of the past—from the Buddha to Schopenhauer, via Aristotle, Chuang Tzu, Epicurus, Epictetus, Montaigne and Spinoza—who have contributed to the eternal investigation into, and practice of, the happy life.

Before embarking on this philosophical journey, I would like to dwell for a while longer on the question of happiness as it arises today. It is evident, and at first sight quite astonishing, that there is a striking contrast between the popular appetite for such questions—widely echoed in the media—and a lack of interest, and even a certain disdain for them, among a large proportion of intellectuals and academics. Robert Misrahi, one of the best commentators on Spinoza, and the author of a fine, personal work on happiness, ponders it in these terms:

> These days we are witnessing a really strange paradox. Even though, in France and throughout the world, everyone aspires to a concrete happiness that can assume myriad forms, philosophy devotes itself to formal studies on language and knowledge, unless, deigning to come down to more everyday issues, it focuses on the tragic sense of life.[7]

What are the reasons for this lack of interest in, and even mistrust of, the question of happiness? How, on the other hand, are we to explain the current favor it enjoys with the general public?

Montaigne and Spinoza forged a new link with ancient philosophy, from a time before Christianity (for which true happiness can be found only in the hereafter); they were the precursors of a modern philosophical quest for happiness. The eighteenth century, which witnessed the Enlightenment, produced countless treatises on the subject: the revolutionary leader Louis Antoine de Saint-Just wrote, "Happiness is a completely new idea in Europe,"[8] and "the pursuit of happiness" is even written into the American Declaration of Independence as an inalienable right. The quest for happiness became more democratic, in tandem with the collective thirst for progress in several different societies.

But in the nineteenth century, while the aspiration to social progress became increasingly important, a critique of the pursuit of individual happiness also emerged. This initially happened within the romantic movement: it was *un*happiness which appeared more authentic, more human, more moving, more creative. There was a vogue for "spleen," seen as the essential source of inspiration, and for an aesthetic of tragedy and suffering, aspects of life that were recognized as praiseworthy and creative. The pursuit of happiness, seen as a bourgeois desire to achieve comfort and peace and quiet, was despised and maligned. Flaubert gave us this ironic definition: "To be stupid, selfish, and have good health are three requirements for happiness, though if stupidity is lacking, all is lost."[9] A more radical critique was then voiced: in the final analysis, the pursuit of happiness didn't seem to be of much use. This was either because it was deemed that a happy life depended solely on individual sensibility (Schopenhauer) or on social and economic conditions (Marx), or because happiness was viewed as a transitory state, "an episodic phenomenon" (Freud),[10] disconnected from any real thinking about one's own existence. The dramas of the twentieth century made European intellectuals even more pessimistic, and the question of anxiety became central to their works (Heidegger, Sartre), while the pursuit of happiness was relegated to outdated utopias.

However, once the great political ideologies had demonstrated their total inability to make the world a better place and had, in their collapse, undermined any belief in progress—that myth on which modernity was built—the question of individual happiness again surfaced, with considerable intensity. This happened first in the 1960s, in the United States, as part of the counter-culture. Through a synthesis of eastern spirituality and modern psychology, the first experiments were made in what came to be known as "personal development," which aimed to increase the individual's creative potential and maximize his or her happiness. Here, the best (such as "positive psychology") rubbed shoulders with the worst (New Age pap, happiness for a dime). Twenty years later, in Europe and especially in France, a new interest in philosophy envisaged as a form of wisdom is emerging. A few philosophers are daring to raise the question of happiness anew, and rethink it: Pierre Hadot, Marcel Conche, and Robert Misrahi, as well as André Comte-Sponville, Michel Onfray and Luc Ferry have all contributed greatly to making this approach popular once more. "If philosophy doesn't help to make us happy, or less unhappy, what's the use of philosophy?" writes André Comte-Sponville.[11] For the same reason, westerners are increasingly curious about the wisdom of the East: Buddhism in particular, for which the question of happiness is crucial. The convergence of these three movements—personal development, philosophical wisdom and an interest in Asian spirituality—is feeding into the new individual quest for happiness and self-realization in a West that has lost its meaning and its collective reference points.

However, most members of the intellectual elite remain skeptical, both for the reasons I have just mentioned (pessimism and the aesthetics of the tragic), to which I do not subscribe, and for reasons that I endorse: the difficulty in grasping a notion that is so elusive, and a certain irritation at the way happiness has been commercialized, turned into something banal and degraded by a flood of feeble and unconvincing works. So it has become de rigueur to mock the quest for happiness and insist that it is necessary for us to be in a bad way, to suffer (the passion of love, for example) if we are to enjoy the moments of happiness life offers us without our having sought them. The essayist Pascal Bruckner, the author of a stimulating critique of the modern quest for happiness, sums it up nicely: "I love life too much to wish to be permanently happy."[12]

I think that there is another reason why certain academics and intellectuals mistrust this theme and are reluctant to tackle it—a reason that they find difficult to admit to: to discuss it properly, we have to expose ourselves on a personal level. We can discourse ad nauseam about language, hermeneutics, the theory of knowledge, epistemology or the organization of political systems without this necessarily involving us intimately. Things are completely different when it comes to the question of happiness, a question that, as we shall see, affects our emotions, our feelings, our desires, our beliefs and the meaning we give to our lives. It's impossible to give a lecture or a talk on this subject without a member of the audience asking, "What about you? What's the meaning of your life? What system of ethics do you follow? Are you happy? Why?" A lot of people find these questions embarrassing.

For my part, I'm not ashamed to admit that the question of happiness interests me for personal reasons, and I have no hesitation about citing examples of psychological and spiritual practices drawn from my own experience. However, I've already referred to those experiences in my *Petit traité de vie intérieure* (*A Short Treatise on the Inner Life*), and so I'll avoid, as much as possible, going over such personal aspects too explicitly; in this book, I will follow the thread of my argument more closely. Nonetheless, it goes without saying that this argument has been woven out of my readings as well as my own life, and it reflects both the intellectual influences that have acted on me and the personal conclusions to which I have come over the more than thirty-five years I have been preoccupied by this question.

CHAPTER 1

Loving the Life You Lead

There's no human condition, however humble or
wretched it may be, that doesn't have a chance for
happiness offered to it every day: to achieve it, all that
you need is yourself.[1]

—Jean Giono

We all find it much easier to answer the question "What
makes me happy?" than to reply to the tougher problem
of "What is happiness?" I can say that I'm happy when
I find myself in the company of the people I love, when I
listen to Bach or Mozart, when I'm making good progress
with my work, when I'm stroking my cat near a nice open
fire, when I'm helping someone come out of a period of
sadness or misfortune, when I'm enjoying a seafood plat-
ter with friends in a small harbor by the sea, when I'm
meditating in silence or making love, when I drink my
first cup of tea in the morning, when I look at the face
of a smiling child, when I'm out hiking in the mountains
or strolling through a forest ... All these experiences, as
well as many others, make me happy. But is happiness
simply the accumulation of such moments? And why do
these moments give me happiness, when they wouldn't

necessarily make everyone else happy? I know people who hate nature and animals, Bach and seafood, tea and long periods of silence. So is happiness merely subjective, is it realized only through the satisfaction of our natural preferences? And why am I sometimes happy to be living through a particular experience when at other times I'm not—when my mind is preoccupied, my body ailing or my heart anxious? Is happiness to be found in our relations with other people and external objects, or rather within us, in a state of inner peace that nothing can disturb?

Of course, it is possible to live well, and even quite happily, without wondering what happiness is, or what can increase it. This is the case, for instance, when we live in a highly structured world where the question of individual happiness hardly arises, where we draw our happiness from the thousand-and-one experiences of daily life, occupying our places and playing our roles in the community to which we belong, and accepting our share of suffering without demur. Billions of people have lived this way and continue to live this way in traditional societies. You need only travel a bit to realize this. It's quite different in our modern societies: our happiness is no longer immediately linked to the "immediate data" of everyday, social life; we pursue it through the exercise of our freedom; it depends more on us ourselves and the satisfaction of our numerous desires—such is the price of our insistence on autonomy.

True, we can also, in the modern world, be more or less happy without asking ourselves too many questions. We seek the maximum of things that give us pleasure, and avoid as far as possible the things that are tiresome or painful. But experience shows that there are sometimes things that are very pleasant for a while, but later produce negative effects, like drinking a glass or two too much, giving into an inappropriate sexual urge, taking drugs, etc. Conversely, disagreeable experiences sometimes enable us to grow, and turn out to be beneficial in the long term: making a sustained effort in our studies or in the practice of some artistic activity, undergoing an operation or taking a nasty medicine, breaking off with people we are emotionally tied to even though they make us unhappy and so on. The pursuit of the agreeable and the rejection of the disagreeable do not always give us accurate bearings when we are trying to lead a happy life.

Life also teaches us that we have within ourselves various brakes that check the realization of our deep aspirations: fears, doubts, desires, impulses, pride and ignorance and so on. Likewise, we cannot control many events that may well make us unhappy: a deadening emotional environment or relationship, the loss of a dear one, a health problem, a setback in our careers ... While we aspire to being happy—whatever this adjective may mean for us—we realize that happiness is something subtle, complex and volatile, and seems totally random.

This is why the scholarly community hardly ever uses the word "happiness." Psychologists, brain specialists and sociologists almost all prefer to talk in terms of a "subjective well-being" that they seek to measure by an index of the "satisfaction" of the lives of those they are canvassing or studying. This state of "subjective well-being" is sometimes a snapshot: it's the state in which people happen to be at the time of the scientific study—when electrodes are placed on their skulls, for example, so as to observe what's happening in their brains while they are

being stimulated in a certain way or carrying out a particular activity. However, scientists recognize that while
biochemical studies and brain imaging make it possible to
gauge pleasure (a simple stimulus), they can never measure happiness (a complex process). So when they want
to talk about a "subjective well-being" that would be
more akin to that complex experience, psychologists and
sociologists have drawn up surveys designed to grasp it
overall, and over a certain period of time: How do individuals assess their lives "overall"? It's not just a question
about one's present sensations. After all, people can feel
a temporary lack of well-being, due for example to an
illness or a professional anxiety that has cropped up the
very same day of the survey, but may still give a positive response to the question if they know that, overall,
they are satisfied with their lives. Conversely, people can
feel moments of well-being within lives that are, overall,
painful.

So, happiness is not a transient emotion, whether agreeable or disagreeable, but a state that needs to be viewed
overall, over a certain period. We say that we are "happy"
or "satisfied" with our lives because, overall, these lives
give us pleasure, because we've found a certain balance
between our various aspirations, a certain stability in
our feelings, our emotions, a certain satisfaction in the
most important areas—emotional, professional, social, or
spiritual. Or we say we are "unhappy" or "dissatisfied"
with our lives if they give us little pleasure, if we are torn
between contradictory aspirations, if our emotions and
feelings are unstable and, overall, painful or if we are
filled with an intense sense of emotional or social failure.

I would add that it is essential to be *aware* of our happiness to be happy. We can reply that we are "satisfied with our lives overall" only if we have reflected on our own existence. Animals may indeed have a sense of well-being, but are they aware of their luck in feeling well? Happiness is a human feeling linked to self-awareness. In order to be happy, we need to be aware of our well-being, of the privilege or gift represented by the good times in life. But psychological studies have shown that we are more aware of the negative than of the positive events that happen to us. The negative events mark us more deeply, and we remember them better. This fact is probably linked to a principle of evolutionary psychology: in order for us to survive, it is more important to detect and remember a danger, so as to find the solution to ward it off, than it is to remember an agreeable event. So we need, as soon as we experience a pleasant, agreeable, joyful moment, to become aware of that sensation, to take it in fully, to cultivate it for as long as possible. This was emphasized by Montaigne:

> Do I find myself in any calm composedness? is there any pleasure that tickles me? I do not suffer it to dally with my senses only; I associate my soul to it too: not there to engage itself, but therein to take delight; not there to lose itself, but to be present there; and I employ it, on its part, to view itself in this prosperous state, to weigh and appreciate its happiness and to amplify it."[2]

Thus, experience shows that becoming aware of our state of satisfaction contributes to increasing our happiness. We savor our well-being, and this reinforces within us the sense of plenitude: we rejoice, we are happy to be happy.

To summarize, I'd say that the psychological or sociological definition of happiness relates to this simple question: Do we love the lives we are leading? And this is the way the question is most often formulated in surveys of individuals' "subjective well-being": "On the whole, are you very satisfied, quite satisfied, not very satisfied, or not at all satisfied with the life you are leading?" This assessment can of course vary over time.

So we can already describe happiness, understood as "subjective well-being," as the awareness of a state of (greater or lesser) overall and enduring satisfaction. But is this sufficient for describing happiness in the full sense of the term? And, above all, is it possible to act on it? Can we make it more intense, longer lasting, more general and less dependent on life's ups and downs?

Finally, we still haven't mentioned the "content" of happiness. Now, as Aristotle points out, "with regard to what happiness is [people] differ, and the many do not give the same account as the wise."[3]

CHAPTER 2

In the Garden of Pleasures, with Aristotle and Epicurus

Happiness involves pleasure.[1]

—Aristotle

Let's continue our philosophical investigation with Aristotle and Epicurus, two Greek thinkers who made happiness one of their main themes. Aristotle was the tutor of Alexander the Great for a few years and a disciple of Plato for twenty years. In 335 BC, at the age of forty-nine, he left his master's Academy to found his own school in Athens: the Lyceum. He was curious about everything and an extraordinary observer: he was interested in biology and physics, in the course of the stars and the organization of political life, in logic and grammar, in education and the arts. He wrote one of the most consummate works on the question of happiness, the *Nicomachean Ethics*, dedicated to his own son. Here, he emphasizes that happiness is always sought for its own sake and never with some other end in view.[2] For him, happiness is the "supreme good." We can seek money for the comfort it provides, and we can seek power in order to win recognition, but happiness is an end in itself. The whole question lies in identifying its nature: What makes us, overall, enduringly happy?

It was mainly through their reflections on pleasure that the notion of happiness was developed by the Greek philosophers. A happy life is first and foremost a life that brings pleasure. Pleasure is an agreeable sensation linked to the satisfaction of a need or a desire. I take pleasure in drinking because I am thereby quenching my thirst, pleasure in sleeping if I am tired, pleasure in learning because I am eager to know, pleasure in acquiring an object I covet and so on. The quest for happiness is an innate human quality and it is probably no exaggeration to state that it is the main driving force by which we are moved. "To be moved" can be taken in a psychological and physical sense: because we feel (or hope to feel) agreeable emotions, we are moved or motivated to act. Pleasure plays an essential part in our biological, psychological, emotional and intellectual lives. Ever since Darwin, biologists have emphasized the importance of the adaptive role of pleasure: the mechanisms linked to it have been selected and preserved because of their central role in evolution. Likewise, for Freud, "what decides the purpose of life is simply the programme of the pleasure principle."[3]

Many of life's pleasures require no effort: enjoying ice cream, satisfying a sexual impulse, getting absorbed in a good TV series. Others require more input: mastering an art, setting out to learn new things, playing a certain sport at a high level and so on. While pleasures vary in intensity and in importance, they are all, always, ephemeral. If we don't continually nourish it with external stimuli, pleasure is exhausted by our enjoyment of it. A nice meal will of course give us great pleasure, but this pleasure lessens as our stomachs fill, and once we have eaten as much as we can, not even the most exquisite dishes can lure us. If certain circumstances (lack of money, illness, loss of freedom) make it difficult for us to indulge in this unsated quest for pleasure, we feel even unhappier, as if lacking in something. Finally, pleasure has absolutely nothing to do with ethics: the tyrant and the pervert take pleasure in torturing others, killing them and making them suffer.

Because it is fleeting, because it needs to be constantly fed, and because it is morally indeterminate, pleasure cannot be the sole guide to a life. We have doubtless already found by experience that the exclusive quest of facile and immediate pleasures brings disillusion in its wake, that the pursuit of diversion and sensory delights never provides us with a full and complete satisfaction. That is why the philosophers of antiquity—such as Speusippus, Plato's nephew and successor at the Academy—condemned the quest for pleasure, and some Cynics thought that the only remedy for suffering was to flee all pleasures. Since they could lead us astray and make us unhappy, we should avoid following our natural inclination to seek these pleasures at any cost.

Aristotle radically rejected such an idea: he began by pointing out that it was only the pleasures of the senses that were subject to this critique: "The bodily pleasures have appropriated the name [of pleasure] both because we oftenest steer our course for them and because all men share in them; thus because they alone are familiar, men think there are no others."[4] But there are many other pleasures than those of the body: love and friendship, knowledge, contemplation, showing ourselves to be just and compassionate and so on. Taking up the saying of Heraclitus that "asses would prefer sweepings to gold," Aristotle points out that pleasure depends on each individual, and he is led to ponder the specificity of human nature. The human being is the sole living being endowed with a *noos*, a Greek word generally translated as "intellect," but one that I will translate instead as "mind," since for Aristotle it means not just intelligence or reason in the modern sense of these terms, but the *divine principle* found in every human being. Aristotle deduces that the greatest pleasure, for human beings, is found in the experience of contemplation, the source of the most perfect happiness:

> If reason is divine, then, in comparison with man, the life according to it is divine in comparison with human life. But we must not follow those who advise us, being men, to think of human things and, being mortal, of mortal things, but must, so far as we can, make ourselves immortal, and strain every nerve to live in accordance with the best thing in us; for even if it be small in bulk, much more does it in power and worth surpass everything. [...] for man, therefore, the life according to reason is best and pleasantest, since reason more than anything else is man. This life therefore is also the happiest.[5]

Aristotle insists that *the pursuit of happiness always constitutes a pursuit of pleasure*, but if the pleasures of the soul contribute most to happiness, he is nonetheless realistic enough to acknowledge that even the wisest person, being human, "will also need prosperity; for our nature is not self-sufficient for the purpose of contemplation, but our body also must be healthy and must have food and other attention."[6] So the secret of a happy life doesn't lie in the blind pursuit of all the pleasures of existence, any more than in renouncing them, but in the quest for the maximum of pleasure with the maximum of reason. It's reason which makes it possible to order our pleasures and lead a virtuous life, the source of happiness: virtue is here defined as a golden mean between two extremes, and is distinguished (as is its opposite, vice) from a natural appetite. Virtue is acquired through reason and is fortified by practice (it is by performing acts of courage that we become truly courageous). So Aristotle states that "happiness is an activity of the soul in accordance with perfect virtue."[7] The greatness as well as the happiness of human beings resides in the way they can become virtuous through their reason and, by deliberate action, cultivate the different virtues: courage, moderation, liberality, magnanimity, gentleness, humor, justice and so on.

A few decades later, another Athenian philosopher, Epicurus, formulated an ethics of happiness based on pleasure. Unlike his predecessor, he did not believe in a divine principle present in humans. In 306 BC, at the age of thirty-five, Epicurus also set up a school: the Garden. Most of his writings have been lost, but luckily we still have a long letter he wrote to a certain Menoeceus, setting out the main aspects of his philosophy regarding the question of happiness.

Epicurus notes that it is essential to eliminate all pointless fears, starting with the two biggest: fear of the gods, and fear of death. He does not deny the existence of the former (probably out of political caution, since his materialist conception of the world makes the existence of any divinities implausible), but he keeps the gods at a distance, explaining that experience shows that they have no influence on human life. So there is no point in praying to them and being afraid of them, presenting them with all sorts of offerings and sacrifices. Likewise we need to rid ourselves of the idea of the soul's immortality, as it introduces the fear of a possible punishment after death. Epicurus borrows from Democritus his idea of a reality composed entirely of indivisible atoms, an approach that underpins his own ethical vision. For him the human being, body and soul, is an agglomeration of atoms that dissolve at death. Epicurus explains that the fear of dying stems purely from our imagination, since so long as we are alive, we have no experience of death, and when we die there will be no individual consciousness left to feel the dissolution of the atoms that make up our bodies and our souls.

Once these two great metaphysical anxieties have been rejected, Epicurus analyses the question of the pleasure that enables us to reach happiness. He starts by noting that our unhappiness results essentially from our permanent dissatisfaction. Then, he makes a first distinction between three sorts of desire: natural and necessary desires (eating, drinking, dressing, having a roof over our heads ...); natural and non-necessary desires (fine cooking, beautiful clothes, a comfortable home ...); non-natural and non-necessary desires (power, honors, great luxury ...). He explains that we need to satisfy only the first group in order to be happy; the second group can be sought, even if it would be better to renounce them; as for the third group, they need to be avoided. "Thanks be to blessed Nature," he exclaims, "who has made it so that necessary things are easy to attain and the things that are difficult to attain are not necessary!"[8] This is what the peasant-philosopher of our own day, Pierre Rahbi, calls "happy sobriety."

We often have a false image of Epicurean wisdom. For many, the label "Epicurean" implies the idea of a life based on the pursuit of the greatest number of, and the most intense, sensual pleasures possible. This perception goes back a very long way, as even in Epicurus' own day, his enemies, envying his success, tried to discredit him by spreading the rumor that his Garden was a place of lust and sensual excess. What was viewed with disapproval in antiquity has become a source of fascination for many of our contemporaries, but it still involves a misunderstanding. In fact, Epicurus conceived of his Garden (a lovely, peaceful spot) as a place where friends could meet, a good opportunity to enjoy others' company and philosophize in a relaxed, cheerful atmosphere, but also to listen to music, or enjoy simple dishes, always in moderation. Indeed, in Epicurus' view, in order to be happy it was imperative to forgo certain pleasures and, at the same time, limit the pleasures people allowed themselves: "And since pleasure is our first and native good, for that reason we do not choose every pleasure whatsoever, but will often pass over many pleasures when a greater annoyance ensues from them."[9]

Epicurus advocated an ethic of *moderation*: a simple diet was better than an abundance of dishes; it was important to flee debauchery and the quest for sensual

pleasure while seeking in all things the health of the body
and the peace of the soul. The supreme virtue, in Epicurean thinking, was prudence (*phronesis*, in Greek): this
made it possible to discern pleasures and pains correctly.
"While therefore all pleasure because it is naturally akin
to us is good, not all pleasure is to be chosen, just as all
pain is an evil and yet not all pain is to be shunned."[10]
Epicurean happiness finds concrete form in what he calls
"*ataraxia*," which means "the absolute tranquility of the
soul." This state can be reached by suppressing imaginary
and superstitious fears, by our ability to find satisfaction
in our basic needs alone and by the quality of our pleasures—friendship doubtless being the most important of
these.

In spite of their metaphysical divergences, what both Aristotle and Epicurus advocate is a *quality* in pleasures that
need to be properly balanced. All excess is to be avoided:
both asceticism and debauchery. We need to nourish and
maintain our bodies and minds properly, as Juvenal's
maxim puts it: "A sound mind in a healthy body."[11] This
balance can be obtained through daily physical exercises
that keep the body healthy while still giving it pleasure.
We need tasty food, in moderation: quality is more important than quantity. We need to pay attention to our
breathing: the schools of wisdom in antiquity offered
their pupils psychological and bodily exercises—we no
longer have the details of these, but they must have been
similar to Asian exercises such as yoga, tai-chi or certain
martial arts, which are in our own day valuable ways of
helping us to be more at ease in our bodies, attentive to
our senses and able to take pleasure in breath, movement,

muscular tension or relaxation. The philosopher Arthur Schopenhauer, who I will be coming back to, stated: "nine-tenths of our happiness depend on health alone [...] a healthy beggar is happier than an ailing king,"[12] and recommended at least two hours' open-air exercise per day, as he correctly believed that we're in a good mood when we feel good in our bodies.

I too have discovered how regenerating it can be for our senses to have contact with nature. When you can go for a walk in a forest, dive into the sea or a river or go hiking in the mountains, while being attentive to the sensations and pleasure this type of experience gives you, you emerge transformed, more tranquil and readier to face life. For this bodily pleasure and sensory regeneration are transmitted to the mind: our anxieties evaporate, our thoughts are clearer and sharper, and our souls, if they were troubled, find peace. Victor Hugo put it well in these lines from his collection of poetry, *Contemplations*:

> Trees of the forest, you know my soul!
> As envy dictates, the crowd praises and blames;
> But you know me well, you have seen me often,
> Alone in your depths, gazing and dreaming.
> You know the stone where a scarab beetle scampers,
> A humble drop of water falling from flower to flower,
> A cloud, a bird can occupy me a whole day,
> Contemplation fills my heart with love [...].

We have almost all had the experience of stretching out in the grass, in our garden or in the park, after a busy day or a week's work. When we arrive, our bodies are tense and our minds preoccupied. But our bodies relax and regenerate in contact with the earth, and our minds quickly benefit from this well-being: in turn, they become empty, tranquil and clear. Given the profound interaction between body and mind, the opposite is also true: when our minds are serene or joyful, our bodies benefit, and we shall see later that it is possible to transform disagreeable emotions—such as fear, sadness and anger—by the strength of the mind.[13]

In Aristotle, as in Epicurus, we thus see a convergence of *hedone* (the pursuit of pleasure) and *eudaimonia* (the pursuit of happiness). This close link between pleasure and happiness has been confirmed by several contemporary scientific studies showing that the experiences which give us pleasure—going for a walk, making love, sharing a nice meal with friends, praying or meditating, laughing, practicing an art or a sport—rebalance the hormonal secretions and the neurotransmitters in our brains, which contributes to the stability of our mood and our "subjective well-being."[14]

CHAPTER 3

Giving Meaning to Life

When a man does not know what harbor he is making for, no wind is the right wind.[1]

—Seneca

Being happy means learning to choose—to choose not only appropriate pleasures, but also our path, our profession, our way of living and loving, as well as our leisure activities, our friends and the values on which we build our lives. Living well means learning to respond to all the demands made of us, to put our priorities in order. The exercise of reason enables us to give a coherent shape to our lives in accordance with the values and goals we pursue. We choose to satisfy a particular pleasure or renounce another one because we give a *meaning* [*un sens*] to our lives—in both senses of the term: we give our lives both a direction and a significance.*

The meaning I am talking about here is not any ultimate, metaphysical meaning. I don't think that it's possible to talk about the "meaning of life" in any universal

---

* In French, the word *sens* can mean both "direction" and "meaning." —Trans.

way, valid for everyone. Usually, the quest for meaning finds expression in a commitment to action, and in one's personal relationships. The building up of a professional career, for example, demands that we identify an activity that suits us and in which we can flourish, and that we settle on a goal and objectives to be achieved. The same is true of our personal relationships: if we decide to have a family and raise children, we organize our lives in accordance with this decision, and our family life gives meaning to our existence. Other people give meaning to their lives by helping those around them, fighting to overcome injustice, or devoting time to those who are underprivileged or suffering. The contents of "meaning" can vary from one individual to the next, but be that as it may, we all come to realize that it is necessary—if we wish to build up our lives—to guide them, give them a direction and a goal, and endow them with meaning.

This dimension appears explicitly in most contemporary surveys on happiness in the form of questions such as "Have you found a positive meaning to your life?" Just as much as pleasure, meaning seems to be essential to happiness. Thus, sociologists place these two factors—pleasure and meaning—among the first factors associated with "subjective well-being." They have also observed that the quotient of pleasure and the meaning we give to our lives tend to converge in any happy individual: if people define themselves as feeling a great deal of pleasure, they will also conclude that they've found a positive meaning for their lives.[2]

The convergence between pleasure and happiness, which the philosophers of antiquity had fully realized, and which is confirmed by contemporary scientific surveys, had to a large extent been denied by twentieth-century psychologists who tended to split the two things apart. As we have seen, Freud showed that human beings are fundamentally driven by the pursuit of pleasure, but he took no interest in the question of meaning. Victor Frankl—a survivor of the death camps, whose thinking was based on that terrible experience—responded by defending a diametrically opposed viewpoint: human beings are fundamentally driven by the pursuit of meaning. Far from contradicting one another, both theories are true: the very nature of human beings impels them to seek both pleasure and meaning. They are truly happy only when their lives are pleasant and also have meaning.

Whether or not we achieve our goals, in fact, is not the essential matter. We aren't going to wait until we've reached all our objectives before we start being happy. The path matters more than the goal: happiness comes as we make our journey. But the journey makes us happier the more pleasure we take in making progress, the more clearly the destination towards which we are moving is identified (even if we have to change tack on our journey), and the more it meets the deepest aspirations of our being.

CHAPTER 4

Voltaire and the Happy Idiot

I have told myself a hundred times that I should be happy if I were as brainless as my neighbor, and yet I do not desire such happiness.[1]

—Voltaire

Do we need to be knowledgeable and lucid in order to be happy? Or, conversely, are not knowledge and lucidity *obstacles* to happiness, especially insofar as the individual endowed with more knowledge and higher aspirations will also have a more demanding conception of happiness and will be more aware of his imperfections than someone with limited aspirations?

Voltaire used a short tale, the "Story of a Good Brahmin," to explore these questions. It's the story of an Indian sage, very lucid and knowledgeable, who is unhappy because he can't come up with any satisfactory answers to the metaphysical questions he keeps asking himself. Next to him lives an ignorant, bigoted woman: "Never in all her life had she reflected for one single moment on one single point of all those which tormented the Brahmin," and she seemed the happiest woman alive. To the question "Are you not ashamed [...] to be unhappy when at your very door there lives an old automaton who thinks about nothing, and yet lives contentedly?" the sage replies, "You are right [...] I have told myself a hundred times that I should be happy if I were as brainless as my neighbor, and yet I do not desire such happiness."

The problem with "happy idiots," indeed, is that such people are perfectly happy so long as they remain ignorant and life hasn't overwhelmed them with problems. But when we reflect even just a little on life, or when it no longer answers our aspirations and immediate needs, we lose that happiness, which is based on mere sensations and the absence of any reflective distance. Furthermore, to deny thought, knowledge and reflection means banishing an essential part of our humanity, and we can no longer satisfy ourselves, once we have realized this, with a happiness based on error, illusion and a complete absence of lucidity. As André Comte-Sponville notes, "wisdom indicates a direction: that of maximum happiness in maximum lucidity."[2] He further reminds us that, if happiness is the *goal* of philosophy, it is not its *norm*. The norm of philosophy is truth. Even if people pursue happiness, those who use their reason will always prefer a true idea that makes them unhappy to a false idea, however agreeable it may be. "If we consider the question of happiness we must consider still more the question of reason," concludes Voltaire in his tale.

This is something important that we have so far not mentioned: illusory happiness does not interest us. Reason allows us to base happiness on *truth*, not on illusions or lies. Of course, we can feel perfectly all right in an illusory or skewed situation. But such happiness is precarious. The happiness of witnessing a cyclist winning a mountain stage in the Tour de France changes into bitterness or disgust the minute we learn that he was on drugs at the time! Or take the example of a woman who falls in love with a married man who has introduced himself as single: this woman's happiness will collapse the minute the truth comes out. After all, who would care to live in the skin of a mad person even if they felt they were as happy as could be? It is through the labor of reason, the exercise of critical discrimination and self-knowledge, that we learn to base our lives on truth.

If I had to give an all-encompassing definition, one that sums up all the characteristics we have just been discussing in these first few chapters, I would say that *happiness is the awareness of an overall and enduring state of satisfaction in a meaningful existence founded on truth.* Obviously, the contents of this satisfaction vary from one individual to another, and depend on their sensibility, their aspirations and the phase of their lives they are going through. Without hiding the unpredictable and fragile nature of happiness, the aim of wisdom is to try and make it as deep and permanent as possible, irrespective of the ups and downs of existence, external events and the pleasant or unpleasant events of everyday life.

But do all human beings aspire to wisdom and happiness?

CHAPTER 5

Does Every Human Being
Wish to Be Happy?

It is impossible to be happy if you do not want to be;
so you need to want happiness and to create it.[1]

—Alain

It has often been claimed that aspiring to happiness is
the most universal of all things. Saint Augustine writes
that the desire for happiness is essential to man; it is the
motive behind all our acts. The oldest and most constant
thing in the world is not just that we wish to be happy,
but that we wish to be nothing *but* happy.[2] Blaise Pascal
drives the matter home: "This is the motive of every action of every man, even of those who hang themselves."[3]
This aspiration is also present in many other cultures.
For example, the French Buddhist monk Matthieu Ricard
notes, in his fine book *Plaidoyer pour le Bonheur* (*Happiness: A Guide to Developing Life's Most Important Skill*),
that "our primary aspiration, that which underlies all the
others, is for some satisfaction powerful enough to nourish our love of life. This is the wish: 'May every moment
of my life and of the lives of others be one of wisdom,

flourishing and inner peace.'"⁴ This seemed so obvious to Plato that he wondered whether the question was even worth asking: "What human being is there who does not desire happiness?"⁵

However, I feel it is necessary to make two important qualifications here. Firstly, this natural aspiration to happiness does not mean that everyone seeks happiness. We can, naturally and as it were unconsciously, *aspire* to happiness without necessarily *pursuing it in a conscious, active way*. There are many people who do not explicitly ask themselves about their happiness, while still pursuing it through the quest for pleasure or the realization of their aspirations. They don't say to themselves: "I'm going to do this or that in order to be happy," but instead aspire to finding concrete satisfactions. The sum and quality of these satisfactions will make them more or less happy. In addition, we can also aspire to happiness without *willing* it—in two ways. First, we can fail to implement the means necessary to achieve happiness (we aspire to being happy, but we don't actually do anything, or not much, to reach this goal); second, and more important, we can deliberately and in full awareness renounce happiness. For not everybody takes happiness to be the supreme value. A value is not the product of a natural need, it is a rational construction; everyone is free to place one value higher than another, even if this means partly sacrificing happiness to this other value—to justice or freedom, for example. Everyone is also free not to wish for happiness and to prefer a roller-coaster life alternating moments of happiness with phases of suffering or spleen. Let's take a closer look at these two points.

•   •   •

We have seen, with Aristotle and Epicurus, that a profound happiness cannot be obtained unless we renounce certain immediate pleasures and think about our choices and our aims. In other words, the pursuit of a fuller happiness demands from us both intelligence and the exercise of the will. If we employ both, we will choose goals that are likely to make us happier, and we will find the necessary means for achieving these goals.

For instance, think of a music lover who dreams of making a profession of music. They devote several hours a day to learning an instrument; they put in the necessary effort to ensure that they master it to a very high degree, even if this means giving up certain pleasures and leisure activities. The more they progress, the more pleasure they will have in playing, and they'll be able to try and make a career in music. If they succeed, they'll be happy to have realized their deepest aspiration, but they will have paid the price through their choices, commitment, perseverance and labor. Other people might harbor the same dream, but cannot organize their lives in such a way as to achieve this goal and will continue to play as mere dilettantes; they'll keep saying to their friends, as the years go by, that they feel they have a "musician's soul," that they would really love to live their passion, but for lack of effort and perseverance these people will never realize their desire and will be condemned to frustration. They won't be really happy, even if they will still feel pleasure whenever they play their instrument.

Others may fail to find happiness because they head off in the wrong direction. Some people don't know that happiness lies in mastering our pleasures and putting them in order of priority: these people become absorbed in a ceaseless and permanently dissatisfied pursuit of immediate pleasures. Others haven't realized that they need to work on themselves if they are to make any progress. This is the case of those unhappy teenagers who suffer from not having a boyfriend or girlfriend but don't take any steps to overcome their inhibitions.

Yet others seek happiness solely through the intensity of sensual pleasure. They concentrate on a pleasure that will suit their tastes, but as this pleasure is ephemeral, they seek to experience it with maximum intensity, to enjoy extreme sensations through sports, music, drugs, alcohol or sex. They always have to go further in their sensations, sometimes so far that they destroy themselves or put their lives in danger. More often, people flee the moments of inactivity that force them back on their own resources, and lose themselves in a permanent hyperactivity, artificially filling the emptiness of their inner lives.

We might also renounce any conscious pursuit of happiness as such because it seems to us so capricious, so random, that it appears futile to exhaust ourselves by seeking it. It's better, we then decide, to strive to get what we love in a more concrete fashion. This might involve, for example, following a certain Epicurean ethics of moderation, just as, conversely, we can choose to live "intensely," deciding, for instance, to drink and smoke to the detriment of our health, to fling ourselves into destructive love-affairs, to allow ourselves to live from moment to moment, even if this means we are forever prone to highs and lows, swinging between fugitive instants of happiness and attacks of melancholy.

CHAPTER 6

Happiness Is Not of This World: Socrates, Jesus, Kant

Blessed are ye that weep now: for ye shall laugh.[1]
—Jesus

In a completely different way, we can abandon the deliberate pursuit of happiness by placing some *ethical value* higher than it—freedom, love or justice, for example—or indeed some whole moral system, with its rules of just behavior. This is what the great German Enlightenment philosopher Immanuel Kant did. For him, happiness is not to be sought as such, but needs to be the result of a moral code: Do what makes you worthy of being happy. The most important thing is that we observe a pattern of behavior that is upright and in line with reason—that we do our duty. If a person has a tranquil conscience, they can feel they are relatively happy, whatever the difficulties they encounter, since they are able to behave in a just manner.

In fact, contemporary surveys show that the awareness of leading a moral or religious life imbued with righteousness is a significant index of happiness. Indeed,

Kant himself seems to have been quite happy to lead a sober, virtuous, well-ordered life, which has made him the despair of biographers eager for spicy details and entertaining anecdotes. He remained a bachelor and almost never left his home town of Königsberg where, for a long time, he was a tutor before becoming a university teacher. Rather paradoxically, he also noted that it is a *duty* for human beings to be as happy as possible, since this means they will not yield to the "great temptation to the violation of duties."[2] He thus turns upside down the Greek view that ethics should serve happiness: for him, it is happiness that should serve morality! Indeed, in his view, full and complete happiness does not exist on earth: it is simply "an ideal [...] of imagination."[3] He concludes that we can reasonably hope to find true happiness only after death (eternal blessedness), as a reward granted by God to those who have managed to lead a just moral life. He thereby agrees with the doctrine of many religions for which a deep, stable and enduring happiness can exist only in the beyond, and will be determined by the quality of our religious and moral lives here on earth.

This belief was already to be found in Ancient Greece: a blessed life in the Elysian Fields was promised to heroes and to the virtuous. It also developed in Egypt and in later Judaism before really taking off in Christianity and Islam. The ideal of sanctity was preferred to that of wisdom. While wise people aspired to happiness on earth, saints aspired above all to felicity in the beyond, in the presence of their Creator.

The end of Jesus' life is a good example of this: because, like all human beings, he aspired to happiness, he had no wish to suffer or to allow himself to be seized by the guards of the senior priests, delivered to Pontius Pilate and put to death. Hence the scene, so full of heart-stopping anguish, on the Mount of Olives, a few hours before his arrest, described by the evangelist Matthew:

> And he took with him Peter and the two sons of Zebedee, and began to be sorrowful and very heavy. Then he said unto them, My soul is exceeding sorrowful, even unto death: tarry ye here, and watch with me. And he went a little farther, and fell on his face, and prayed, saying, O my Father, if it be possible, let this cup pass from me: nevertheless not as I will, but as thou wilt.[4]

In spite of his anguish, Jesus still agrees to make a free gift of his life, as he intends to remain faithful to the voice of the truth guiding him (the voice of the one he calls his "Father") instead of saving himself and fleeing as his disciples had suggested. He has sacrificed his earthly happiness out of fidelity to the truth and to a message of love that contradicts the religious legalism that places the rigor of the Law above all else.

The end of Socrates is quite similar to that of Jesus insofar as he also refused to flee, but drank the hemlock, a deadly poison, and thus obeyed the judges who had condemned him to death. This happened to be an unfair sentence, but Socrates did not want to disobey the laws of the City, since in his view every citizen had to submit to them. In the name of his own values, he renounced happiness and life. Socrates—who in some ways was more like a saint than a wise man—was in any case wary of the word *happiness*. According to Plato, he preferred to seek a "good" life, based on reason and founded on values such as the good, the beautiful and the just, rather than pursue a "happy" life that might well not be in line with justice: don't tyrants, egotists and cowards also tend to pursue happiness?

If Jesus and Socrates sacrificed their lives to a truth or to values higher than earthly happiness, they believed in and aspired to a supreme happiness after death. Jesus was convinced that he would rise after death to experience eternal happiness with God in the life to come. The Apocalypse, the last book of the Christian Bible, describes the "Heavenly City," a metaphor for eternal life: "Behold, the tabernacle of God is with men [...]. And God shall wipe away all tears from their eyes; and there shall be no more death, neither sorrow, nor crying, neither shall there be any more pain: for the former things are passed away."[5] Socrates was also certain that there was a place of happiness for the just in the next life.[6] In short, what they were seeking was a *deferred* happiness.

This is not always the case. There are people who don't believe in a life after death and who are ready to sacrifice their lives in the name of an ideal higher than happiness. How many have given up happiness in order to fight oppression and injustice? When he stood in front of the tanks on Tiananmen Square in June 1989, the young Chinese student who was risking his life made the struggle against the dictatorship his supreme value and hoped simply that his gesture would further the cause of freedom. The same was true of Nelson Mandela in South Africa, and is true of all those who risked or sacrificed their lives—and continue to do so—for a cause that in their view transcends them and is worth more than their individual happiness.

This raises a twofold question for us to answer. First, to what extent do these heroic actions, insofar as they

respond to the deepest aspirations of the individuals concerned, give them a certain happiness? While they suffer
at having to lose their lives, are not Socrates and Jesus at
the same time happy because they are giving their lives
for a noble cause and, in so doing, are they not acting in
accordance with their deeper nature?

CHAPTER 7

On the Art of Being Oneself

In sense of personal being lies
A child of earth's chief happiness.[1]

— Goethe

Gustave Flaubert was an implacable observer of human nature, and scrutinized the deeper motives that lead people to act in accordance with their inner nature. He describes the core of egotism that underlies the pursuit of our aspirations and the realization of our actions.

From the idiot who wouldn't give a sou to redeem the human race, to the man who dives beneath the ice to rescue a stranger, do we not all seek, according to our various instincts, to satisfy our natures? Saint Vincent de Paul obeyed an appetite for charity, Caligula an appetite for cruelty. Everyone takes his enjoyment in his own way and for himself alone. Some direct all activity toward themselves, making themselves the cause, the center, the end of everything; others invite the whole world to the banquet of their souls. That is the difference between prodigals and misers: the first take their pleasure in giving, the second in keeping.[2]

To be happy means, firstly, to satisfy the needs and aspirations of our being: a person inclined to silence will seek solitude, someone who likes to talk will seek the company of others. Just as birds live in the air and fish live in water, everyone needs to move in the atmosphere that suits them. Some humans are designed to live in the noise of cities, others in the tranquility of the countryside, while others need both. Some are designed for manual activity, others for intellectual or artistic work, while others prefer to focus on relationships. Some need to set up a family and aspire to an enduring life as part of a couple, while others like different relationships throughout their lives. People can never be happy if they go against their deeper natures.

Education and culture are valuable as they inculcate in us the need for limits, laws, and respect for others. It is essential not just for us to know ourselves, but also to test out our strengths and weaknesses, to correct and improve within us those things that can be changed, but without trying to distort or thwart our deepest being. And education and culture can sometimes prevent us from developing our own sensibilities, they can lure us away from our vocation and our legitimate aspirations. This is why we sometimes need to learn how to become ourselves irrespective of the cultural and educational schemata that have sometimes turned us away from what we are. This is what the Swiss psychologist Carl Gustav Jung called the "process of individuation," which often happens when we hit forty and for the first time assess our lives overall.

We may then discover that we are not fully ourselves, that we are seeking to please other people without showing ourselves enough respect, trying to create an ideal or artificial image to win love or recognition; we may find that we have been leading an emotional or professional life that doesn't fit what we really are. Then, we seek to discover our true individuality and pay more attention to our own sensibility.

"In sense of personal being lies / A child of earth's chief happiness,"[3] wrote Goethe. For events don't count as much as the way each of us experiences them. Developing our sensibility, strengthening our character, honing our gifts and our tastes—these count more than the external objects that may give us pleasure. We may be tasting the finest wine in the world and derive no pleasure from it if our nature is allergic to wine or if we haven't sharpened our senses of taste or smell sufficiently.

Happiness consists in living in accordance with our deeper nature, developing our personality so that we can enjoy life and the world with the richest sensibility we can. Some children may be extraordinarily happy with a single basic toy if they have been able to develop their imagination and creativity, while others will be bored by a hundred sophisticated toys if they constantly need new objects to derive pleasure from.

CHAPTER 8

Schopenhauer: Happiness Lies in Our Sensibility

Our happiness depends on what we are.[1]

—Schopenhauer

The German philosopher Arthur Schopenhauer, a contemporary of Flaubert, took up Goethe's idea and went even further: he was convinced that our nature predisposes us to be happy or unhappy. For him, it is our sensibility (these days, we would say our genes) that determines our aptitude for happiness or unhappiness. The first condition for being happy seems to be ... having a happy temperament! A cheerfulness of character, he says, will "determine our capacity for sufferings and joys."[2] Plato had already drawn a distinction between grouchy (*duskolos*) temperaments, who don't rejoice when they meet with favorable events and are annoyed by unfavorable events, and cheerful (*eukolos*) temperaments who rejoice at favorable events and are not annoyed by unfavorable events. These days, we would say that there are "glass half-empty" and "glass half-full" people.

"Our happiness depends on *what we are*, on our

individuality, while in general we take account only of our fate and *what we have*," continues Schopenhauer. And he adds, with that sardonic humor so characteristic of him: "Fate can improve, and frugality does not require much from a person: but an idiot remains an idiot and a country bumpkin remains a country bumpkin for all eternity, even if they were surrounded by houris in paradise."[3] The only thing we can do is learn to know ourselves so as to lead lives that are as attuned to our natures as possible. But, for Schopenhauer, we cannot change: an angry person will continue to fly into a rage, a fearful person will always be a coward, an anxious person forever anxious, an optimist an optimist, just as a sickly person will always be sickly and a force of nature always a force of nature, and so on. Schopenhauer distinguishes between:

- What we are: personality, strength, beauty, intelligence, willpower ...;
- What we have: belongings and possessions;
- What we represent: social position, reputation, glory.

For most people, the two last points seem the most important: it is often thought that happiness depends mainly on what we possess and on the importance we have in the eyes of others. This is not the case, says Schopenhauer: permanent dissatisfaction, competition, rivalry, vicissitudes, the vagaries of fate and so on will soon have ruined our happiness if it is based solely on *what we have* and *what we seem*. For him, happiness resides fundamentally in *what we are*, in our being, in our inner contentment, the result of what we feel, understand and wish for: "What someone possesses for himself, what accompanies him in solitude and that nobody can give to him or take from him, is much more essential than all that he possesses and all that he is in the eyes of others."[4]

I share this vision, but only partly. Experience does show that happiness is intimately bound up with our sensibility, our character and our personality. Certain individuals are much more inclined than are others to be happy: because they have good health, because they are optimistic and cheerful by nature, because they spontaneously look on the bright side of life, because they have a well-balanced emotional make up, and so on. I also support the claim that it is our intimate disposition that makes us happy or unhappy much more than do our possessions or our successes. What has enabled me to be happier through the years is not so much social or material success—even if this has helped—as the *inner work* that has enabled me to improve, to bind the wounds of the past, to transform or move beyond beliefs that made me unhappy, but also to grant myself the right to find complete fulfillment in my personal and social life, a right that for a long time I would not give myself. But it is here that I part company with Schopenhauer. While he is right to emphasize that happiness stems essentially from sensibility and personality, he greatly underestimates the way we can, by working on ourselves, shape our own sensibilities, making them more able to flourish, and thereby manage to realize our deepest aspirations.

In fact, in Schopenhauer there is a curious contradiction: he postulates a quasi-genetic determinism and at the same time proposes rules of life to make us happier! Probably because he was pretty unhappy throughout his life, Schopenhauer hopes in wisdom more than he believes in it. He was sickly from childhood onwards and was profoundly affected by the suicide of his father when he himself was seventeen; all his life he would suffer intensely from severe frustrations in his emotional life. The first was an unrequited love for an actress, which came as a violent disappointment to him. During the writing of his masterpiece *The World as Will and Representation*, he had a liaison with a chambermaid who gave birth to a stillborn child. Then he had to abandon plans to marry a woman who had fallen seriously ill. Later, he fell in love with a singer who could not bring her pregnancy to term. After this, he gave up any plans to marry. But his professional life gave him no more joy. In spite of all the hopes he had placed in his book, it attracted no interest and sank without trace for over thirty years. His university career was also a source of cruel disappointment to him: his classes were regularly cancelled ... as nobody turned up. Sick at heart, he was forced to give up teaching. This helps us understand his pessimistic vision of life even if we don't necessarily share it.

I have had the opposite experience and found that one can, through psychological and spiritual exercises, change the way one looks at oneself and the world. So, like Schopenhauer, I think that happiness and unhappiness are in us, and that even "given the same environment, everyone lives in a different world."[5] But, unlike him, I am convinced that we *can* change our inner lives.

Thousands of sociological studies of happiness have been published over the past thirty years or so, especially in the United States. Their conclusions are no different from those we have just mentioned. They can be summarized as follows:

- There is a genetic predisposition to being happy or unhappy.
- External conditions (geographical environment, place of residence, social standing, marital status, wealth or poverty and so on) do not have much influence on the matter.
- We can be happier or less happy by modifying the perception we have of ourselves and of life, and by modifying our view of things, our thoughts and our beliefs.

Professor Sonja Lyubomirsky, who runs the Department of Psychology at the University of California, Riverside, states that approximately 50 percent of our aptitude for happiness seems to come from the sensibility of the individual (genetic factors) and 10 percent from our surroundings and external conditions, while 40 percent stems from personal efforts.[6]

CHAPTER 9

Does Money Make Us Happy?

No one will be happy if tormented by the thought of
someone else who is happier.[1]

—Seneca

In a period of economic crisis, when an increasing number of people are suffering from uncertainty, and when I
myself am earning a decent living, I hesitate to write that
money doesn't necessarily make one happy. We know the
piquant request made by Jules Renard: "If money doesn't
make *you* happy, then hand it over to me!" Nonetheless,
most sociological studies carried out across the world
tend to demonstrate that money is not a defining factor
in individual happiness. In 1974, the American econo-
mist Richard Easterlin published a famous and disturbing article in which he pointed out that while the gross
income per capita in his country had made a huge leap
of 60 percent between 1945 and 1970, the proportion of
people who thought of themselves as "very happy" had
not changed in the least (40 percent). The noteworthy rise
in income and the dramatic changes in lifestyle linked to
the increase in material comfort had no appreciable impact on the satisfaction of individuals. This article stirred

up unease in economic circles, as it threw into question one of the most deeply rooted beliefs of Americans, for whom economic prosperity is a main cause of happiness. As the magical formula of liberal capitalism decreed: rise in GDP = increase in individual and collective well-being.

Official statistics in France reveal the same thing: between 1975 and 2000, while there was an increase of over 60 percent in GDP, the proportion of people declaring that they were "quite satisfied or very satisfied" with their lives stagnated at around 75 percent. The statistics are even crueler in other European countries. In Great Britain, for instance, while national wealth has almost tripled in half a century, the proportion of individuals who view themselves as "very happy" fell from 52 percent in 1957 to 36 percent in 2005.

Another way of tackling the question consists in comparing the index of life satisfaction in very wealthy countries with that of poorer countries. It might be imagined that people are happier in rich countries than they are in poor or so-called developing countries. But this is not the case: the level of satisfaction is the same in the United States or Sweden as it is in Mexico or Ghana, while the revenue per inhabitant of these countries differs by a factor of one to ten.

Surveys bring out another interesting phenomenon: the defining role of social comparison in happiness—in other words, the sociological application of the celebrated words of Jules Renard: "It's not enough to be happy; other people have to be unhappy!" The way we assess our own situation is influenced by comparing it with that of other people living near us or in a social environment close to ours. Our happiness seems to be relative, compared to that of other people. "To be poor in Paris means to be poor twice over," as Émile Zola noted. The researcher Michael Hagerty, of the University of California, Davis, has shown that the residents in towns where there is a big gap in incomes have a quota of happiness less than those who live in towns where incomes are pretty similar: the comparison with the top of the sample (those who earn the most) increases the dissatisfaction of those who earn less. Another study, this time carried out among students, indicates that a large majority of them (62 percent) would feel "happier" at landing a first job bringing in $33,000 per annum if they knew that their peers had got $30,000 jobs than if they had got a $35,000 job while knowing that the others would be earning $38,000![2]

This reveals how harmful it can be when there is too great a disparity in income within the same society, not only because it creates frustration, but because the globalized media can also have a hugely negative impact on the happiness of individuals who are increasingly inclined to compare their belongings with those of others, not only in their immediate environment, but on a planetary scale. And since it is impossible for everybody to enjoy the lifestyle of the wealthiest, dissatisfaction is endemic in individuals who, had it not been for these comparisons, might have been quite satisfied with their lot.

This shows how important it is, if we are to be happy, to avoid measuring ourselves against those who are happier or more prosperous! The Stoic philosopher Seneca summed it up in the neat formula quoted at the beginning of this chapter: "No one will be happy if tormented by the thought of someone else who is happier."[3] Actually, Seneca counted money among the things he thought it was "preferable to have." Like Aristotle, he felt that it was better to have plenty of belongings than to be deprived of them. But like most philosophers of antiquity, he also viewed too great an abundance of possessions not only as not being necessary to happiness, but as potentially harmful because of the anxieties inherent in wealth: the fear of being robbed, the significant amount of time required to manage one's goods, other people's jealousy and so on. La Fontaine's fable "The Cobbler and the Financier," in which a humble cobbler receives an unexpected gift of a hundred crowns, a gift which ends up ruining his peace of mind, illustrates this perfectly. A lack of money can obviously stop you from being happy by forcing you to focus all your energies on survival activities and preventing you from realizing your true aspirations. Admittedly, a minimum amount of money contributes to happiness, but the ceaseless pursuit of enrichment is just as damaging. If we are not to become the slaves of money, said the sages of antiquity, we need—once we have satisfied our basic needs—to limit our material desires in order to spend more time with our families, our friends, our passions and our inner lives.

Surveys bring out an interesting paradox here. When people are asked, "What are the things that seem to you the most important for happiness?" money and material comfort do not figure among the main factors. On all continents, people vote for family, health, work, friendship and spiritual life as the pillars of happiness. We should note in passing that this last point counts for little in France, though it's important in the many countries where religious faith is more deeply rooted. In the United States, for example, people who practice a religion seem to be happier and live on average seven years longer than others (they have fewer problems with alcohol, drugs and depression, and fewer suicides and divorces).

But when respondents are asked, "What are the things that you would like to have in order to be happier to-day?" most reply "money" (just ahead of health). Why do we feel that money would enable us to be happier when we also reckon that it is less decisive than family, friend-ship or health, for example? Individuals who are rich but in poor health, or deprived of affection, will definitely be less satisfied with their lives than those with modest incomes, good health and many friends. I can see three explanations for this.

The first is that we aspire to what we do not have and naturally include the increase of material well-being if we don't have it. Most of the people who answer surveys are in pretty good health and doubtless quite satisfied with their emotional and professional lives. But they think that they would be happier if they had what they seem most cruelly to lack: money. And this is particularly true as we experience the most severe crisis of the post-war period while living in a world that is constantly stimulating our desire for possessions. The endless plugging of goods in adverts and the display of other people's wealth even-tually whet our material appetites to an unreasonable degree, and the need for money becomes urgent. A few recent studies, which still need confirmation, are also starting to demonstrate a link between happiness and economic growth.[4] Even if we have a roof over our heads and food on our tables, we may suffer from not being able to go away on vacation or to afford a tablet com-puter. In the mid-eighteenth century, Jean-Jacques Rous-seau was already pointing out that we very quickly get used to the comfort made possible by technical progress. What were, to begin with, mere *commodities* quickly turn into *needs*, and people "would have been unhappy at the loss of them, though the possession did not make them happy."[5] What would he say these days, when living without a car, without a television, without a computer or a mobile phone would seem unthinkable to the vast majority of those who have already acquired such objects?

The second reason for the paradox mentioned above is that we are going through a period of great uncertainty. We are much more "insecure" than our parents who, in France, enjoyed the "Thirty Glorious Years" that followed the end of the Second World War: these days, almost nobody is safe from unemployment and a greater or lesser degree of job insecurity. The need for money is making itself felt not only among those who are struggling to make ends meet, but also among those who want to provide themselves with a margin of security in the face of an uncertain and anxious future.

Finally, money represents much more than the mere acquisition of material goods. It can also help us to slake our passions, to travel and to live in a more independent fashion. All of these are excellent reasons for desiring money not as an end in itself, but as a means for making our lives easier and also helping us, sometimes, to realize our deeper aspirations.

CHAPTER 10

The Emotional Brain

If you can change your brain, you can change your life.[1]

—Rick Hanson

The twentieth century witnessed some fabulous scientific discoveries both in the field of the infinitely big (astrophysics) and in that of the infinitely small (quantum physics), as well as in the life sciences. However, one continent remained more or less unexplored: the human brain. But in the past thirty years, it has been the object of many studies. The twenty-first century will certainly see the secrets of its complexity laid bare, and even, quite probably, produce a better understanding of the way our minds work and interact with our bodies.

Initial research has already brought to light the extraordinary chemistry of the brain, a chemistry that has a direct influence on our well-being. For example, it has been discovered that certain molecules produced in the encephalon play an important part in our emotional balance. Over sixty neurotransmitters (or neuromediators) occupy the center stage of the brain.[2] These substances derive from amino acids and ensure communication from one neuron to another thanks to the influx through the nerves, by encouraging or inhibiting the propagation of signals. The effects of neuromediators differ with the zone where they go into action. An excess of one neuromediator may imply a lack in another. Each lobe receives from the nervous system electrical influxes that it then proceeds to convert into chemical messages, and this transformation is responsible for harmony in the brain. Neurotransmitters are hampered by an unbalanced diet, emotional upset and a lack of sleep.

The neurobiologist Eric Braverman has used the Brain Electrical Activity Map (BEAM) test to study the electrical functioning of the brain.[3] Invented in the 1980s by researchers in the Faculty of Medicine at Harvard, this brain imaging technique makes it possible to examine whether the brain is balanced or unbalanced in dopamine, acetylcholine, GABA (gamma-aminobutyric acid) and serotonin. Dopamine corresponds to energy and motivation, acetylcholine helps creativity and memorization, GABA relaxes and brings mood stability and serotonin is linked with enjoyment of life and a sense of satisfaction. According to Braverman, these four main neuromediators in the brain have a major influence on our behavior.

Thus, people who have a good balance of GABA will tend to be benevolent and caring; they will also be able to meet problems with a certain detachment. This neurotransmitter is also involved in the production of endorphins, molecules that are released by physical effort (sport or sexual intercourse), creating a sensation of euphoria. But if there is too much GABA in the brain, there will be an inclination in the person to make sacrifices on behalf of others and become dependent on them. Conversely, a severe lack of the same neurotransmitter can create a certain instability and a propensity to lose self-control.

Dopamine, mainly secreted by the frontal lobes, is identified with an appetite for life, motivation and decision-making. When dopamine predominates, the personality is lively and extroverted, likes power but may find it difficult to accept criticism. In excessive amounts, the molecule can lead to impulsive, violent acts.

Acetylcholine, produced in the parietal lobe, is linked to creativity, intuition, sociability and a taste for adventure, as well as to the memory. When there is too much of it, it can give rise to an excessive altruism; people with this problem may even think that those around them are taking advantage of their kindness, and become paranoid. A lack of this substance makes us lose our sense of reality and ability to concentrate.

Serotonin, which is found in the raphe nucleus and even in the small intestine, is involved in enjoyment of life, optimism, contentment, serenity, sleep and the harmonizing of the two hemispheres of the brain. In excessive amounts, it can create considerable nervous tension and a lack of self-confidence: people affected will feel attacked by the least criticism and will be pathologically panic-stricken at the thought they might arouse the displeasure of others. Because of a lack of serotonin, such people will feel rejected by their friends and will withdraw into themselves: depression is a frequent symptom of a lack of serotonin.

As well as being affected by the neurotransmitters, the brain is influenced by the hormones, substances secreted by the endocrine glands such as the pituitary, the thyroid, the adrenal glands and the genital glands. They can also be produced by the pancreas, which secretes insulin; as well as by the hypothalamus, which secrets oxytocin: we shall be coming back to this.

Released into the blood by endocrine glands and organs, hormones are then generally bound to a protein that regulates their action in order to ensure the proper functioning of a good number of physiological functions such as cell metabolism, sexual development and the way the body reacts to stress. Finally, like a key fitting into the right keyhole, the hormone latches onto the receptor that corresponds to it, situated on its target organ, and thereby helps the organism to adapt and face the needs that may occur.

Among the hormones that play a role in well-being and positive emotions are oxytocin, which is released in orgasm, childbirth and breastfeeding. This polypeptide plays a positive role in our ability to trust others; it favors empathy and generosity and motivates us to offer help to others. Oxytocin also reduces the stress and anxiety that can be felt in social situations.[4]

The hormone system regulates itself via a feedback mechanism that encourages or slows down the production of hormones. But they are often disturbed by stress, as well as by disruptive elements that undermine, block or modify the action of a particular hormone, creating harmful effects. These undesirable agents include mercury and lead, but also bisphenol A and the phthalates found in various plastics present in our immediate environment, and the parabens that are used to make certain cosmetics as well as industrial foodstuffs and hundreds of pharmaceutical products.

Another factor in well-being that has recently been highlighted by brain specialists is the length of a gene (5-HTTLPR) that determines the production of a molecule responsible for transporting serotonin. The length of this gene varies with individuals and has a far-from-negligible influence on our moods. One recent study in the United States, based on a sample of 2,574 people, has shown that a short gene, with fewer transporters than a long gene, makes the subject more sensitive to stressful events, while a long gene makes people better able to remember positive events.[5]

So our emotional lives are considerably influenced by our brains and by all the chemical substances secreted by our bodies. These substances play an important part in our aptitude for happiness or unhappiness, as Schopenhauer had surmised, though at the time he had no knowledge of the chemical functioning of our organisms. But while we may come away with the impression that neuromediators and hormones determine our behavior, various scientific studies have shown that we can also act on them by gradually altering our habits and behavior. An extraordinary neuroplasticity has recently been discovered: the brain is constantly changing itself, in accordance with our experiences, by producing new neurons or new neural connections.

Contemporary science shows that our aptitude for happiness is influenced by our genetic inheritance and by the chemical secretions of our organism, while not being entirely fixed by them, since it can change if we alter our diets, our behavior and our lifestyles. It thus finally puts paid to the often-proposed hypothesis of genetic determinism. The quest for the "happiness gene" is a pure fantasy. True, our genes do condition, to a significant degree, our disposition to happiness, but they do not completely determine it. They largely form the basis of our emotional structure, but we can act on our emotions and our states of mind. This was well understood and explained over three hundred and fifty years ago by a Jewish Dutch philosopher by the name of Baruch Spinoza, as we shall see at the end of this work.

CHAPTER 11

On the Art of Being Attentive ... and Dreaming

While we are postponing, life speeds by.[1]

—Seneca

We have already emphasized that the quality of our awareness of happiness is in itself a defining factor in that happiness. The more aware we are of our positive experiences, the more our pleasure and well-being increase. As a reflexive act, awareness enables us to "savor" our happiness: in return, this makes happiness itself more intense, profound and enduring. Just as decisively, our happiness is nourished by the quality of attention we bring to bear on what we are doing. The Stoic and Epicurean sages of antiquity had underlined this crucial point and claimed that a single instant touched on eternity. Happiness can be enjoyed only in the present instant. Again, scientific studies have confirmed this point that many philosophers and psychologists have long been trumpeting. Thanks to brain imaging, researchers in the neurosciences have established that the zones of the brain activated when we concentrate on a single experience are different from

those activated when our minds are wandering or ru-
minating over various thoughts.[2] Clinical observation
has also revealed that subjects suffering from nervous
or depressive illnesses often operate in a mode of "rumination," unlike people who display a notable subjective
well-being, who move more frequently from one activity
to another while remaining attentive to what they are doing. So a link has been demonstrated between attention/
concentration and well-being, and between rumination/
mind-wandering and malaise, and these states of mind
have been shown to be rooted in the brain.

Various therapies have, with very convincing results,
been applied to patients suffering from depressive illnesses: these patients are encouraged to learn how to live
while paying attention to the present moment. Among
these therapies we find, for example, the practice of so-
called "mindfulness" meditation developed by American
psychiatrist Jon Kabat Zinn some twenty or so years ago
and inspired by the basic elements of Buddhist meditation. The experience of silent meditation makes it possible
to fix your attention without tensing it, to quiet the mind,
to calm the ceaseless round of thoughts, and to recharge's
one's inner batteries. Given the interaction between body
and mind, this new tranquility has an effect both on the
organism and on our emotions. Specific studies have been
carried out on trained meditators such as the aforementioned French Buddhist Matthieu Ricard, who has been
meditating for several hours a day for almost forty years;
these studies have revealed that these meditators experience a specific brain reaction: their gamma waves are
much more intense than those of other subjects, and a
"better synchronization of the overall electric activity
in the brain" is observed in them, as well as "an increase

in neuro-plasticity, i.e., in the propensity of the neurons to establish more connections."[3]

If the regular practice of meditation can help us to live "mindfully," every experience in daily life can also, of course, be a source of well-being, producing similar effects. We simply need to be attentive to what we are doing at the present moment: our sensations when we are cooking a meal, when we are eating, when we are walking, when we are working, when we are listening to music and so on, rather than performing these tasks or occupations while thinking of other things or allowing our minds to wander from one worry to another. Every moment in daily life can then become a source of happiness, not only through the pleasure we take in these different activities, but also because attention stimulates our brains in such a way that they in turn produce waves or substances that intensify our impression of well-being.

We discover that, very often, we are not living in the present, but allowing our thoughts to drift to the past or the future. We carry out several tasks at the same time. We brood over various worries while we are working. Modern life forces us to be hyperactive and only intensifies these tendencies which lead to an exponential increase in stress, chronic fatigue, depression and anxiety in our societies. But if we pay closer attention to what we are doing, to our sensations, to our perceptions, the way we are carrying out our actions—then we can change our lives.

However, I need to make two significant qualifications to what I've just said. All the studies dealing with wisdom or personal development do indeed insist on this crucial point,[4] but they don't mention a complementary aspect that strikes me as just as essential. While our modern lifestyle fosters mental dispersion, in which our thoughts escape the present moment, and thus produce stress and malaise, it cannot be a question, either, of falling into the opposite excess by attempting to banish all reverie and all wandering of the mind. In order to be balanced, our minds do indeed need to be concentrated and attentive, but they also need to be able to roam around without any precise goal, just following their moods, inspirations and associations of ideas. This is what we experience in the nightly world of our dreams, which compensate for our controlled and conscious daily activities. Likewise, it's no bad thing, at certain times of the day, after we've been concentrating particularly hard on our work or our everyday activities, to allow ourselves moments when our attention can relax and our minds float, frolic, allow themselves to be carried along by the flow of thoughts that come and go. This kind of "dilution" of awareness is different from the "rumination" that usually consists of concentrating on some remorse about the past or some anxiety about the future, and increases our negative emotions. Montaigne tells us that this was one of the main reasons for the pleasure he took in going out for a ride on his horse: horse riding encourages reverie.

I find it noteworthy that many children have difficulties with paying attention, and are hyperactive and edgy. More often than not, these children are forever being bombarded by external stimuli: they have to focus at school, and their home environments are dominated by TV, computers and interactive video games. There is no longer any room or free time for them to build an inner life. Such an inner life is created from thinking and from education—but also from the reverie and games in which children give free rein to their imaginations. "Too many stimuli from the outside world inhibit the creative impulse of children, preventing them from expressing themselves, finding their own words and making innovations," explains the clinical psychologist Sevim Riedinger. In her view, playing games remains—in spite of the world of computers—an

> essential basis for children to build up a sense of being. This is where, in perfect freedom, and outside any constraints, they can savor an inner space that belongs to them. This enables them to make, unmake and remake their reality, and to absorb its challenges. They can then seek solutions from further away and from higher levels, when they've reached a dead end. They can put things in perspective and view things with fresh vigor.[5]

When we are adults we are so in thrall to external stimuli and the many tasks we have to perform that, most often, we also have to function in "think" and "concentrate" mode. We too end up by being stifled and drying up.

So our minds need both to concentrate and pay attention, and to relax and regenerate through inner silence—the result of meditation, for example, as well as through reverie, allowing our minds to wander—and imagination. Inactivity and silence, listening to music, reading poetry, contemplating nature and works of art: these are all valuable ways of fortifying our inner lives. Usually, as with children playing games, it is by relaxing our minds that we can enable the solutions to our problems to suddenly pop up, and find the brightest ideas, the intuitions

that will help us advance further down a road that had
been blocked before. Certain therapies, indeed, consist in
placing the subject in a modified state of awareness that
enables the brain to function in a different mode from
the habitual rational one, favoring the emergence of re-
pressed emotions. In traditional societies, this is typically
the experience of the shamanic trance, an experience that
Greeks and Romans found in the initiatory mystery cults.
The western world has drawn inspiration from these
methods, still common in several traditional cultures, and
uses them to develop therapies based on modified states
of awareness and interference with our mental processes:
hypnosis and rebirth therapy are good examples. When
human subjects are destabilized, their brains can no longer work in accordance with the habitual mode of control, and they can then evolve, cross inner boundaries,
and move to another "state of being."

The second important qualification I'd like to make
is this: while our happiness depends a great deal on our
ability to live in the present moment, it is also reliant
on our capacity to remember the happy moments in our
lives. If our minds wander into the past, they can make
us unhappy when they dredge up negative memories, remorse and regret—but they can give us a rare happiness
when they dig up happy times. Happiness is nourished by
the awareness of being happy, and while this awareness
is always activated in the present, it also stimulates the
realm of the imagination to seize on and "treat" memories
from the past. In his novel *In Search of Lost Time*, Proust
wrote lyrically of the happiness that this or that exhumed
memory can give us in the present. But even in antiquity,
various philosophers had already emphasized this point.
When, in his *Philebus*, Plato refers to the pleasures of the

soul, he insists on the role of memory, referring especially to the happiness given by the memory of bodily pleasures, and the corresponding anticipation of pleasures still to come. It is because I have retained the memory of the intense pleasure I had in drinking a fine wine that I'm happy not just to remember it, but also to look forward to tasting it again. Epicurus, too, insists on the essential role of memory as an aid to happiness, especially when the body is suffering from illness or abuse. What allows us, on such occasions, to rediscover *ataraxia*, a profound sense of inner peace, is the memory of moments of happiness. But it is not just a question of the mind taking a trip into the past: as in Proust, memory allows us to relive a pleasant sensation; it is again in the present that happiness is experienced thanks to this reminiscence.

I would also add that if memory contributes to our happiness—but also, sometimes, to our unhappiness—this is because it leads us to situate our lives within a certain duration. And if we take an intense pleasure in living the moment, we also remember, even without our activating it explicitly, all our past experiences, all the ties of emotion that link this moment to so many others, as well as to our fellow human beings. This is what lies at the basis of our identity—and herein lies the drama of Alzheimer's. A few years ago, I completely lost my memory for ten hours or so (amnesic ictus); I then realized that this aptly named "absence" entails a form of depersonalization: no longer able to recognize anyone, lacking any memory of our life stories, we are as it were cut off from ourselves; no pleasure in the moment will then be able to give a decisive sense of a "self"-awareness that endures over time.

CHAPTER 12

We Are What We Think

I do feel that [life] is a grim, painful, nightmarish, meaningless experience and that the only way that you can be happy is if you tell yourself some lies and deceive yourself.

—Woody Allen

An old philosophical debate that has been given a new lease on life by modern psychology involves the link between our emotions and feelings on the one hand, and our thoughts and beliefs on the other. Do the former precede and condition the latter? Or is it rather that our emotions and feelings are the result of our thoughts and beliefs? Take a concrete example: Are sad people who doubt their capacities sad because they have the idea or the belief that they are just losers—or have they developed such a belief because, as children, they experienced a traumatic emotion that, making them feel sad, has given them an inferiority complex?

The ancients tended to think that thought was prior to, and governed, emotion. "We are what we think," claimed the Buddha. Since Spinoza and then Freud, the moderns have, however, emphasized the importance of emotions, which, in their view, determine the content of our thoughts. But with the development of positive psychology at the end of the twentieth century, our contemporaries have again underlined the decisive role of thoughts and beliefs in our emotional lives.

I think this is a false problem. The fact of the matter, in my view, is that there is a permanent interaction between emotions and thoughts, and they condition each other mutually. Sometimes emotion precedes thought: ever since I got bitten, I've been scared of dogs and think they're dangerous. Sometimes thought precedes emotion: my mother told me that dogs are dangerous and I'm paralyzed by fear when I see one coming my way. What matters is that, in both cases, we can act on our emotions to develop our thoughts and beliefs, just as we can act on our thoughts and beliefs to regulate our emotional lives.

Most of the new behavioral therapies, which generally produce good results, associate working on our emotions with working on our thoughts, in a positive reprogramming. Body and mind, emotions and thoughts are mobilized to enable us to get over a trauma, a phobia, or some wound from the past. But working on our thoughts and emotions is not simply curative; it can also be preventive. We then need to be vigilant when this or that thought or emotion appears, so that we are not disturbed by it. If we pay attention to our inner lives, and draw on the resources of introspection, we will more and more quickly recognize what is being played out within us, and react before the thought or the emotion becomes rooted in us and starts to cause trouble. This is also one of the main benefits of meditation: by daily distancing ourselves from our thoughts and emotions, we learn to no longer identify ourselves with emotions that arise at the wrong moment, and we are no longer overwhelmed by every little thought. We learn to stop saying "I'm angry" or "I'm sad"; instead, we note, "Ah, here comes anger, or sadness." By putting things at a distance, we are better able to control our emotional lives and vigilantly select among the thoughts that come to our minds.

We can take this one step further and actively work on our thoughts and beliefs. We will be all the more inclined to do so once we have realized that the outer world is simply the mirror of our own inner world. When businessmen and -women look at a landscape, they see a site to be developed; poets see, as did Baudelaire, a "forest of symbols"; lovers think of those they love and dream of going for a walk with them; melancholy folk nostalgically cast their minds back to far distant events in a natural framework like the one before their eyes; cheerful souls are enthused by the colors and harmony of the landscape; and depressives see nothing more than a gloomy spectacle. Our thoughts and our beliefs, like our states of mind, determine our relationship to the world. Confident people see a great opportunity in a given situation where the more timorous will focus on the risk they will run. People who respect themselves will have no doubts about the esteem others have for them, while individuals who have lost all self-esteem will be sensitive to the slightest negative sign, which will then merely intensify their negativity.

The ancients already understood this perfectly. After the Buddha, the Stoic sage Epictetus stated that nobody can harm us if we don't want them to—everything depends on the judgment we ourselves make of the bad things that happen to us.[1] I'll be coming back at greater length to the wisdom of the Buddha and the Stoics. What matters here is showing how essential it is to work on our thoughts and beliefs if we are to build a happy life for ourselves. Schopenhauer understood this clearly and insisted, for example, on the need to develop our positive thoughts while eliminating our old negative beliefs. In his treatise *The Art of Being Happy*, he advises us to "consider what we possess with exactly the same eyes as if it were taken away from us"[2] (material goods, health, social position, love affairs), as it is often only after we have lost something that we realize how lucky we had been. We move from the thought "And what if I had that?" to the thought "And what if I lost that?" We look at those who are worse off than ourselves rather than those who are in a better situation—for, as contemporary sociological studies have confirmed, comparison is one of the keys to happiness and unhappiness.[3] Schopenhauer also recommends that we avoid as much as possible having too many hopes and fears.[4] On the other hand, the contemporary philosopher André Comte-Sponville has built his whole philosophy of happiness on the theme of the wisdom of despair: "The sage has nothing more to hope nor to fear. Because the wise are entirely happy, they lack nothing. And because they lack nothing, they are entirely happy."[5]

Martin Seligman, a professor at the University of Pennsylvania, runs the Positive Psychology Center there. For forty years, he has been one of the pioneers in positive psychology, a disciple that investigates optimal human functioning and aims to enhance those factors that enable individuals to flourish. Rather than focusing on illness or malaise, this discipline highlights the origins of good psychological health. Within this framework, Seligman has undertaken several studies designed to understand what promotes health or illness, happiness or unhappiness. These studies, spread over several decades, and involving thousands of individuals, have led him to bring back the old distinction between "optimistic" individuals, who tend to see the positive side of things and look confidently towards the future, and the "pessimists," who are inclined to see the negative side of things and are anxious about the future. These studies, complemented by the work of several other researchers, have shown that "optimists" perform better overall than "pessimists" in every area, and are thus much more likely to be happy. Because they have confidence in life and look with serenity to the future, they "attract" to themselves, as it were, more positive events and encounters than do the pessimists. They also enjoy better health, are eight times less prone to depression, and have more hope in life.[6] In any difficult situation, while the optimist can find a solution to the problem, the pessimist remains convinced that there isn't one, or that the critical situation is going to last. Basically, the pessimist doesn't think that happiness is possible. He agrees with Woody Allen that life is "a grim, painful, nightmarish, meaningless experience and that the only way that you can be happy is if you tell yourself some lies and deceive yourself."

So why is it that some individuals are more optimistic while others are more prone to pessimism? Seligman proposes various factors, the main one being the sensibility of the individual as transmitted through their genetic inheritance. But the influence of parents and teachers can't be neglected, nor can that of their general environment and religion. So some ethnic groups seem to be more optimistic than others—Americans, for example—while the French are reputed to be among the most pessimistic people in the world. The influence of the media is also decisive: they can sustain an atmosphere of anxiety by using their headlines to point to everything that's wrong with the world. While it is probably difficult for a typically "pessimistic" individual to become "optimistic" overnight, each of us is nonetheless able to attenuate the negative character of our beliefs and thoughts while approaching life with greater confidence. We will become all the happier, perhaps; or, if not, we will at least feel less unhappy.

CHAPTER 13

The Time of a Life

Ah, the joy of this task that nobody ever completes: living![1]

—Christian Bobin

"Are you happy?" Formulated in such an abrupt manner, this question always makes me uneasy. If it's an inquiry about my current state, it's not of any real interest: I may be feeling ill at ease in the television studio where this question is fired at me and feel like replying "no" because of this temporary malaise, even though I am, overall, happy in my life, and vice versa. If it's a question about my general state over a period of time, it has the problem of being too either/or, as if we were completely happy or, conversely, totally unhappy. In fact, we are almost all "more or less happy," and our impression of happiness fluctuates with time. I may decide that I'm generally happy today, in other words satisfied with the life I'm leading, and certainly much happier than ten or twenty years ago; but perhaps I will be happier or unhappier in ten years. The aim is to be more deeply and enduringly happy, as much as life allows us.

•   •   •

The researchers who have analyzed the different parameters of subjective well-being note that there is, in each individual, a sort of "fixed point" of happiness linked to his or her personality. Each individual possesses, as a matter of nature, a certain aptitude for happiness. People will find themselves below their fixed point when they have to confront a difficult situation (illness, professional issues, emotional problems), but above this point when they experience a positive event (marriage, promotion). However, they will almost always return to their fixed point. Some studies have even shown that most of the people who win the lottery experience a peak of happiness for a few months, before gradually returning to their previous level of well-being. Conversely, many people who become handicapped as a result of a serious accident are extremely unhappy for a certain period of time, and often even long for death; but their enjoyment of life and the feeling of getting better gradually take the upper hand and, after an average of two years, they generally go back to their "fixed point," the constant level of happiness that they felt before their accident.[2]

The interest of working on ourselves and seeking wisdom consists entirely in managing to raise our "fixed point" of satisfaction so that happiness becomes more intense for us, deeper and longer lasting. I myself have discovered that it is possible to break through to new levels in my ability to be happy. These are so many "hands" in the game of cards we are dealt that constitute the new "fixed points" in our aptitude for happiness.

In addition to this subjective development, linked to our inner work on our own individual selves, there is also a life-long rise in the index of satisfaction that is found to a somewhat similar degree in a majority of people. Indeed, statistical studies show that most people share an index of satisfaction that varies in a regular way with age. In France, for example, drawing on surveys that have asked people every year since 1975 to rate their levels of satisfaction with life, researchers at the National Institute of Statistical and Economic Information have demonstrated that there was a real "age effect," whatever generation was being canvassed. Generally speaking, the overall index of satisfaction with life continues to diminish from the age of twenty until people start to enter their fifties, after which it experiences a notable rise until around the age of seventy, when it undergoes a new phase of decline.[3] The statisticians can't really give any explanation for this phenomenon. In my view, we could hazard the hypothesis that the lowering of overall satisfaction until one's fifties corresponds to the loss of illusions and the need to confront the difficulties of adult life and the host of questions about the shape one's life has taken that can be observed in most individuals between thirty-five and fifty. The sharp rise that follows, from around age fifty to around age seventy, can be explained by the mellowness of maturity: we are increasingly satisfied with our professional lives and, with experience, we have acquired a knowledge of ourselves and others that enables us to live more fully. Sometimes we have reestablished our lives on new values or new desires. Some people have even "remade" their lives. The gradual decline in the index of satisfaction from the age of seventy on could be explained by the rigors of aging—increasing health worries, the loss of our physical and intellectual abilities and the approach

of death—as well as the death of friends and sometimes of
our partners.

In fact—and we have so far not emphasized this
enough—our happiness depends to a great extent on our
relationship with others.

CHAPTER 14

Can We Be Happy Without Other People?

Without friends no one would choose to live, though he had all other goods.[1]

—Aristotle

Can happiness result from a life governed entirely by egotism? Without necessarily hurting others, we can take no interest in them and concentrate exclusively on the increase of our own personal well-being. However, contemporary sociological studies show that love, friendship and emotional ties constitute one of the main pillars of happiness (along with health and work). Aristotle and Epicurus had already emphasized this: there is no real happiness without friendship. Indeed, Aristotle did not draw a distinction between conjugal love and friendship: for him the same feeling is found in both, involving identity and reciprocity, which unites spouses as it does friends, and comprises their happiness. There is identity, because we recognize our friend first and foremost as "another self" with whom we share the same aspirations, the same tastes and interests, the same values and sometimes the same plans for our lives. We are happy at having found someone with whom we feel in communion on essential things.[2] Diogenes Laertius relates that when Aristotle was asked what a friend was, he used to reply: "A single soul residing in two bodies."[3] Montaigne said the same when describing his friendship with Étienne de la Boétie: "And at our first meeting [...] we found ourselves so mutually taken with one another, so acquainted, and so endeared betwixt ourselves, that from thenceforward nothing was so near to us as one another."[4] And there is reciprocity, because, if we are to blossom and flourish, love needs to be shared: if we love someone who doesn't love us, the result can only be our unhappiness. I will add to these two dimensions a third, which is more implicit in Aristotle: otherness. What touches us in the other person is also that person's radical and irreducible difference, what is unique about them, their own face. We rejoice at the singularity of our friends, and also at their freedom, and we want these things to grow ever stronger.

Love as friendship (*philia*), which Aristotle discusses, implies the presence of a dear person with whom we like to make "common cause": we may share with them a passion for the arts, for sports or games, or intellectual endeavors, or we may wish to set up a home with them. Indeed, Aristotle notes that "of friends made with a view to pleasure, also, few are enough, as a little seasoning in food is enough."[5]

Nobody can be happy without love, in other words without having an experience of emotional communion. However, this does not mean that every form of love makes us happy. Passionate love is based on physical desire and, more often than not, on an idealized representation of the other, and so it can also make us very unhappy.

After all, there is something pathological in passionate love: we idealize our partner, are drawn into games of seduction, suffer jealousy, undergo sadness and euphoria in succession, hopes and disillusionments ... Many love affairs begin with a prologue of passion before evolving into a deeper knowledge of the other person, a friendship with an element of complicity—with the result that love becomes enduring and happy.

Of course, in every emotional relationship there is both egocentric love and altruistic love: we are simultaneously concerned with ourselves, in the love we give and receive, and preoccupied by the other's pleasure, happiness and self-fulfillment. These two aspects are mingled in very diverse ways. Love is all the more intense and radiant if the friends/partners love each other with the reciprocity of a powerfully altruistic love. But we should not make ourselves unhappy by trying to give others more than we can. Montaigne condemned the spirit of sacrifice found in some Christians and emphasized the need not to overstep the limits of our nature by trying to love or help others: "He who abandons his own particular healthful and pleasant living to serve others therewith, takes, in my opinion, a wrong and unnatural course."[6]

Most modern thinkers have decided that human beings are visceral egotists who, even when they are apparently acting in a disinterested way, are really pursuing their own interests. This was the view of Thomas Hobbes and Adam Smith, and it was adopted by Freud. This pessimistic conception of human nature was perhaps inherited from the Christian dogma of original sin, according to which human nature is basically corrupt and can be restored only by divine grace. If we take God away, only pessimism is left! However, this view rests on a truth we have already mentioned: there is a kernel of egotism that inclines us to act according to our nature in the pursuit of our aspirations and the fulfilling of our actions: a generous person takes pleasure in giving just as the miser takes pleasure in keeping. But there is another law of the human heart, just as universal, it would seem, but unknown to those pessimistic thinkers: by working for the happiness of others, we also make our own happiness.

Several scientific studies have shown that there is a link between happiness and altruism: the happiest people are those who are most open to others and feel just as much—or even more—concern for the fate of others as they do for their own.[7] There is no conflict between the love of self and the love of others, between being happy and making others happy. Quite the opposite: taking an interest in others reduced egotism, which is one of the main causes of unhappiness.

Even if the word "altruism" was invented in the nineteenth century (the French word *altruisme* goes back to Auguste Comte), what it refers to—love/giving—and its direct relationship to happiness had already been highlighted by many sages, mystics and philosophers. Plato was already noting in the *Gorgias* that "the happiest man is the one who has no trace of wickedness in his soul." The Apostle Paul reports a saying of Jesus that is curiously missing from the Gospels, even though it expresses their quintessence: "It is more blessed to give than to receive."[8] Jean-Jacques Rousseau states: "I know and feel that to do good is the truest happiness the human heart can savor."[9] In our own day, Matthieu Ricard, echoing the tradition of Buddhism that goes back for more than two millennia, concludes his most recent work, *Plaidoyer pour l'altruisme* (A Plea for Altruism) with these words:

> True happiness is inseparable from altruism, as it forms part of an essential goodness that is accompanied by the deep wish that everyone may flourish in their lives. It is a love that is always available and that proceeds from simplicity, from serenity and from the immutable strength of a good heart.[10]

As against the doctrine of original sin, I fully share the opinion of Matthieu Ricard and Buddhism: human nature is fundamentally good, and our hearts are designed to blossom in loving and giving. When we commit negative acts inspired by hatred, anger and fear, we often have the impression of being, as it were, outside of ourselves: after all, when someone is furiously angry, we say they are "beside themselves." On the other hand, when we perform positive actions motivated by goodness, altruism and empathy, we feel that we are fully ourselves. This is because we are by nature fundamentally inclined to altruism. It is reactions to the vicissitudes of life that lead us to develop fear, anger and even hatred. To escape these, it is often good to work on ourselves, our thoughts and our emotions. But nothing can replace the experience of being loved. Loving cures us of many of life's wounds: not only when we are loved, but also when we discover the treasures of goodness buried within our own hearts. We can then enter the extraordinary virtuous circle of life: the more we help others, the happier we are; the happier we are, the more we feel like helping others.

CHAPTER 15

The Contagiousness of Happiness

Each man and each woman should think continually of this: happiness, by which I mean the happiness we win for ourselves, is the finest and most generous of offerings.[1]

—Alain

In spring 2013, I took part in a round table discussion at the Fes meetings in Morocco organized by Faouzi Skali. The theme was happiness. When I had finished speaking, André Azoulay, the King of Morocco's adviser, responded. This just man is a Jew who has always taken a forceful role in Israeli-Palestinian dialogue. He expressed his skepticism about the pursuit of individual happiness in a world marked by so much suffering. Without saying it in so many words, he was raising a question which has long preoccupied me: Can we be happy in an unhappy world? I will reply unhesitatingly: yes, a hundred times yes. Because happiness is contagious. The happier we are, the happier we make those men and women around us. What would be the point of giving up all personal happiness out of empathy or compassion for those who are suffering, if this is not of the slightest use to them? What matters is not refusing to be happy, it's acting and committing ourselves to making the world better, and not creating our own happiness at the expense of others. And what really is scandalous is building up a financial empire and not sharing any, or not much, of one's fortune. Or basing our success on others' unhappiness. Or, to a lesser degree, taking no account of the common good. But if we place our success or prosperity at the service of others, if our happiness then allows us to bring happiness to others, we can then conclude that it is a moral duty to be happy. In his *Fruits of the Earth*, André Gide expressed it eloquently:

> There are on this earth such immensities of misery, distress, poverty and horror that the happy man cannot think of it without feeling ashamed of his happiness. And yet no-one can do anything for the happiness of others if he cannot be happy himself. I feel an imperious obligation to be happy.[2]

Scientific studies have provided clear confirmation: happiness spreads. "Happiness is genuinely contagious," states Nicholas Christakis, professor of sociology at Harvard University and author of a study of nearly five thousand individuals that lasted for twenty years. "People's happiness depends on the happiness of others with whom they are connected. This provides further justification for seeing happiness, like health, as a collective phenomenon"— so says the study, which even points out (and the details may raise a smile) that every happy friend increases our probability of being happy by 9 percent, while each un-happy friend makes our capital of happiness drop by 7 percent.[3] For if our happiness plays a part in others' happiness, the converse is also true: unhappiness, too, is contagious.

This contagiousness of happiness is something we can all experience through the cinema or the media. When, for example, we are watching TV and see sports person-alities showing their happiness at winning a major trophy, we are affected by the sight even if we are not particularly concerned. I will never forget the rapture that seized the whole of France after the World Cup final in 1998: people were kissing strangers in the streets and all social barri-ers fell for a few hours, swept away by this great wind of shared rapture. We are also moved, sometimes to tears, when we see on TV the absolute happiness of a father or mother finding a lost child again, the friends and family of freed hostages hugging them after years of separation, a gravely ill child suddenly recovering and so on.

However, some people are irritated at the sight of another's happiness, especially when it is their rivals who are concerned. They can then sometimes take pleasure in the discomfiture or failure that affects someone whom they see as a competitor on the professional level or a rival in emotional terms. According to biologists, this attitude—more frequent than one might think—was an adaptive advantage in evolution: the elimination of a ri-val facilitated the survival of an individual or allowed that individual to obtain a better place within the group. Buddhism explains that this spirit of rivalry is a poison that makes happiness dependent on others in a negative spiral: happy when they fail, unhappy when they succeed.

It shows that one of the keys to serenity consists in ceasing to compare ourselves with others, leaving behind the spirit of rivalry, and seeking to overcome any jealousy. The best antidote to this poison is learning to take pleasure in others' happiness.

CHAPTER 16

Individual Happiness and Collective Happiness

> When each man most seeks his own advantage for
> himself, then men are most useful to one another.[1]
> —Baruch Spinoza

"We prefer to be happy rather than sublime or saved,"[2] writes Pascal Bruckner in his critical essay on the modern pursuit of happiness. In his view, this began with the Enlightenment, when western modernity replaced the religious quest for the heavenly paradise with the search for earthly happiness. "The earthly happiness is where I am," as Voltaire put it in his poem "Le mondain" ("The Man of Society") in 1736.

While it's true that western agnosticism has replaced the quest for heavenly beatitude with seeking happiness on earth, it is not true to say that happiness is "a western, historically dated value"[3] that developed with the modern period. The pursuit of happiness here below is a universal quest that goes back much earlier. It even considerably predates the birth of Christian theology. We find an expression of it in a narrative that goes back to the third millennium BC, *The Epic of Gilgamesh*, one of the most ancient texts of mankind. The story denounces the hubris inherent in the quest for immortality and emphasizes the importance of the quest here on earth for a happiness that lies within our grasp. Likewise, Ancient Egyptians pursued happiness in the here and now as much as in the hereafter, and the concept of earthly happiness is strongly attested to in the Hebrew Bible. As we have seen throughout this book, the quest for individual, earthly happiness is also found in the philosophers of antiquity: Aristotle, Epicurus and the Stoics in particular. It exists in the great Asian civilizations, India and China, as well, and it is the very essence of Buddhist teaching. In short, while Pascal Bruckner is correct to emphasize the major break represented by the modern era, he seems to be forgetting that the advent of the Christian world itself marked a very clear break with most forms of ancient wisdom. The modern quest for finding perfection through working on ourselves has indeed replaced the Christian quest for sainthood by means of asceticism and grace, but it also goes back two millennia, before Christianity, and joins the ancients' quest for wisdom, as well as the wisdom of the East. While there is a difference between contemporary forms of the quest for happiness and those promoted by the ancients, this difference doesn't lie in the pursuit of individual happiness here and now, but in something else altogether: the separating of the individual good from the common good.

For the sages of antiquity, as indeed for eastern thought, solitary happiness does not exist. Since the Greeks believed that political harmony was more important than individual equilibrium, it was not conceivable in their view for anyone to be happy without taking an active part in the good of the city. The Stoics linked the happiness of the wise to their commitment and civic spirit. This enabled them to participate in maintaining the order of the world. The individual happiness extolled by Plato, Aristotle, Confucius and the Buddha could be conceived of only as part of a holistic vision in which the individual was not separated from the group, from the city, from the community. For one thing, this was because spirituality and philosophy presuppose a common effort, a transmission, a form of mutual aid, and are essentially practiced within a group: the Buddhist *sangha*, the spiritual leadership of Stoicism, the friendship of Epicureanism. For another thing—especially for the Greeks—it was because the common good was perceived as higher than individual happiness and required everyone to work for the good of the city. Thus, Aristotle stated clearly that "even if the end is the same for a single man and for a state, that of the state seems at all events something greater and more complete whether to attain or preserve."[4]

The philosophers of the eighteenth century and the founders of our first Republics shared this point of view fully. The individual happiness promised by the leading figures of the Enlightenment and noted in the American Declaration of Independence was part of a larger project of collective happiness. Improving individual well-being and improving society went hand in hand. The eighteenth and nineteenth centuries were borne along by an amazing belief in the progress of human societies that could be brought about by the exercise of reason, science, education and law. The emancipation of the individual and the pursuit of personal happiness were still linked with the great republican ideals of liberty, equality and fraternity, and everyone aspired to a better world, even if the obtuse self-interest of nations and their expansionist designs led to the terrible conflicts of the twentieth century.[5] The great collective ideals did not, however, disappear, and in the wake of the Second World War the desire to change the world was still able to galvanize hundreds of millions of people. The Communists believed in a potentially ideal society for the coming of which they fought. From Dr. Schweitzer to the Abbé Pierre,* socially concerned Christians were committed to improving the conditions of other human beings, and the hippies of the counter-culture brandished the slogan "Peace and Love" on their banners.

Mass consumption and the revolution in lifestyle that took place at the end of the 1960s marked a profound shift. There was an accelerated extension of individual freedoms within the context of a society now in thrall to an exacerbated consumerism. Individuals, now increasingly preoccupied with themselves and the satisfaction of their desires, devoted most of their efforts to increasing their material comfort and achieving social success. This rise of a new form of individualism marked a major break: the link between individual happiness and the common good was destroyed in our modern societies, especially in France.

In his essay *L'Ère du vide*[6] (The Era of Emptiness), Gilles Lipovetsky has offered a remarkable analysis of this second individualist revolution. While the individual who was produced by the first revolution (the advent of modernity) was still imbued with great collective ideals

* Founder of the Emmaus movement.

and a lively interest in public affairs, contemporary individualism is nothing more than a form of narcissism. We are all now preoccupied solely by the quest for our immediate pleasure, our personal success and the defense of our own interests. Egocentrism, indifference to others and to the world have become, for many people, the norm. The novels of Michel Houellebecq contain an astute description of this narcissistic individualism: his characters are apathetic, egotistic, frustrated, cynical, the adepts of a joyless hedonism and a disabused narcissism. The slogan of this type of individualism could be: "*Après moi, le déluge.*" Though we crave ever more possessions, we are nonetheless aware of the limits and dangers of the mercantile logic that governs the world: but, convinced that there is no point in working on behalf of everyone, we are caught in a deadly logic that transcends our grasp and, forced to confront our fears and our impotence, all that is left to us is to give free rein to our instinctive desires in a sort of passive nihilism. This is an unprecedented situation.

However, although these forms of behavior still dominate, we have, for a good ten years or so, been witnessing the birth of what I would call the "third individualist revolution." For something did start to change at the end of the 1990s and the beginning of the 2000s with, concomitantly, the rise and democratization of personal development, eastern spirituality and philosophy as a form of wisdom, and also the birth of the anti-globalization movement and the appearance of social forums, the development of ecological awareness and the rise of various solidarity initiatives across the world: these include microcredit, social finance and, more recently, the Indignados movement. These various movements reveal a need to give meaning back to life—both to personal life (by working on ourselves and by asking existential questions) and to the life we share, through a new impetus to the great collective ideals.

These two quests, indeed, often seem very closely linked. It is often the same people who carry out psychological or spiritual work on themselves who are also sensitive to ecology, join humanitarian associations, take part in citizens' actions and so on. The era of the split between the political or humanitarian militant, exempt from any spiritual preoccupation, on the one hand, and the New Age meditator, solely concerned with improving his or her karma, is to a great extent already a thing of the past. For many people, spiritual and planetary preoccupations, a concern with ourselves, and an awareness of the world all overlap. Admittedly, this trend is still in the minority. Narcissistic individualism and consumerist ideology are still predominant in the West. But these "weak signals" that are appearing throughout the world constitute a coherent alternative to the logic of destruction; they show that the quest for individual happiness is not inevitably separate from involvement in political life and a concern with the common good.

The two things, in fact, go together. We have already seen that individual happiness is contagious. The utilitarian thinkers who advocate "the greatest happiness of the greatest number" have also emphasized that nobody can be lastingly happy in a dangerous world in which the security of goods and persons cannot be guaranteed. This can take place only in a society where people are happy. The interest of each also lies in the happiness of all.[7]

CHAPTER 17

Can the Quest for Happiness Make Us Unhappy?

There is only one duty: making ourselves happy.[1]
—Denis Diderot

Pascal Bruckner is much more convincing when he denounces "the imperative of happiness" that is endemic in our contemporary societies, showing how, since the end of the Second World War, the quest for happiness has gradually been transformed into a command to be happy. The "right" to happiness has changed into a "duty," and thus into a burden. Modern people are "condemned" to be happy and "have only themselves to blame if they fail. [...] We are probably the first societies in history to make people unhappy about not being happy. [...] The Christian drama of salvation and damnation is echoed by the secular drama of success and failure."[2]

Actually, the obsession with happiness often thwarts happiness. One reason is that a mercantile society dangles before us many fake promises of happiness linked to the consumption of objects, physical appearance and social success. Those who yield will soon be stumbling from one unsatisfied desire to the next, and thus from one frustration to another. Another reason is that contemporary hedonism often comes at the price of an expensive asceticism. Happiness—like salvation in bygone days—has to be deserved. As the German sociologist Max Weber showed, the Protestant Reformation "took rational Christian asceticism and its methodical habits out of the monasteries and placed them in the service of active life in the world."[3] Henceforth, the sacred has to be written in accordance with the grammar of the profane: the discipline followed by monks in order to ensure their salvation has gradually mutated into another form of constraint, to which everyone must conform if they are to attain happiness. This is the asceticism of the broker who slaves away night and day in order to grow rich—the ultramodern figure of the Puritan capitalist entrepreneur depicted by Weber. It's the asceticism of the marathon runner, the sporty type who haunts the gym, and all those who practice sport at a high level (physical exercise, indeed, often seems like the modern equivalent of the spiritual exercises of the ancients). And, quite simply, it's the asceticism of parents who have to juggle demanding jobs, children, hobbies, friends—and finally end up exhausted by their desire to do everything at the same time.

Finally, American studies have often highlighted the way that happiness is the result of our setting our goals too high for us ever to achieve them ... starting with the goal of being very happy! They confirm the work of the French researcher Alain Ehrenburg on "the weariness of the self." Combining a history of psychiatry with a sociology of lifestyles, Ehrenburg has shown that many of the forms of depression that currently affect westerners (chronic fatigue, insomnia, anxiety, stress, indecision ...)

are the price that needs to be paid for the twofold imperative of autonomy and self-fulfillment. Depression, a veritable "pathology of responsibility," is the symptom of the individual freed from all religious and social tutelage who still aims to live up to the modern imperative to find self-realization.

> In 1800, the issue of the pathological individual appeared with the madness-delirium pairing. In 1900, it was transformed by the dilemmas of guilt that shook the person made nervous by her desires to free herself. In 2000, the pathologies of the individual involve the responsibilities of a person who has freed herself from the laws of her fathers and the old systems of obedience and conformity. Depression and addiction are the two sides of the sovereign individual.[4]

This analysis brings out very clearly the extent to which the modern injunction to happiness can simply make us more unhappy.

However, should we abandon the quest to be happy? Does the correct attitude, if we are to obtain happiness, lie in expecting nothing, wishing for nothing, hoping for nothing? Letting life go by without giving ourselves any aims, or pursuing any ideal of any kind? Admittedly, we can be happy without ever raising the question of happiness, and sometimes even this question alone can complicate our lives. A Brazilian friend told me that, for a long time, she had lived with a certain nonchalance, satisfied with her life. And then one day, a woman friend who was coming to live in France had asked her, "Are you happy?" And my friend concluded: "I'd never asked myself that question and suddenly I lost all joy in living, as this question tormented me!"

At the same time, as the great Scottish philosopher David Hume notes, "The great end of all human industry, is the attainment of happiness. For this were arts invented, sciences cultivated, laws ordained, and societies modelled, by the most profound wisdom of patriots and legislators."[5] The whole of history is made up of dreams or utopias drawn up by individuals and societies. It is because human beings have sought a better life and done all in their power to achieve it that all the progress of mankind has been accomplished. The same is true of our personal lives: it's because we want to make progress, to be happier, that our lives improve and give us ever more satisfaction. The obsession with happiness or the quest for a too-perfect happiness can produce the opposite result. The art of happiness consists entirely in not setting goals that are too high, unattainable and overwhelming. It's a good idea to set more gradual goals, to reach them step by step, to persevere without getting stressed while being able sometimes to let go and accept life's failures and ups and downs. Montaigne and the Taoist sages understood this clearly and expressed it well: we need to allow our attention to act effortlessly; never to confront a situation with the aim of forcing it; to be able both to act and not to act. In short, to hope for happiness and pursue it while being supple and patient, without any excessive expectations, without stress, with hearts and minds in a state of constant openness.

CHAPTER 18

From Desire to Boredom: When Happiness Is Impossible

Life swings like a pendulum backwards and forwards
between pain and ennui.[1]

—Schopenhauer

The aim of natural selection is the survival of the species,
not the happiness of individuals. In order to adapt and
survive, we have developed three abilities that may be
obstacles to individual happiness:

Custom is an adaptive quality that enables us to tolerate something annoying and repetitive. However, it has
two drawbacks: we may become accustomed to a certain
unhappiness and stop seeking for happiness; and conversely, we can become accustomed to well-being and lose
our awareness of our happiness.

This phenomenon is intensified by the fact that, in
order to ward off dangers more effectively, we become
more aware of *negative* events than of positive events.
Our brains are made to detect problems and focus on
them rather than to dwell on positive events.

Finally, *dissatisfaction* makes us strive constantly for

more and better things: this is how human beings have ceaselessly tried to improve their lot. Now, this adaptive quality may well become an obstacle to happiness when we prove to be permanently dissatisfied.

Let's dwell on this last point, which is definitely the most important and has attracted the attention of all philosophers who have been led to reflect on the question of happiness. When we assuage a need or a desire, we of course experience a real sense of satisfaction: I am hungry and am glad to eat; a child hankers after a toy and is satisfied to possess it; an employee is happy to obtain a long-desired promotion; and so on. But these satisfactions are of short duration, since new cravings soon arise.

> But whilst the thing we long for
> Is lacking, that seems good above all else;
> Thereafter, when we've touched it, something else
> We long for; ever one equal thirst of life
> Grips us agape.

So the Roman philosopher Lucretius, a follower of Epicurus, astutely points out.[2] Human beings are perpetually dissatisfied, and stagger from desire to desire. Like Kant, we can then identify happiness, in other words a deep, enduring and overall happiness, with the assuaging of all our inclinations and all our aspirations. "Happiness is the satisfaction of all our desires, extensively, in respect of their manifoldness, intensively, in respect of their degree, and protensively, in respect of their duration."[3] But such a happiness cannot, of course, exist, and Kant draws the logical conclusion that happiness is not to be had on earth. As we have seen, like Plato he situates happiness in the beyond. For noble and upright souls, true happiness will always remain something to be hoped for while we are in this life; we must not pursue it, but make ourselves worthy of it by our virtuous actions or by the sanctity of our lives.

Schopenhauer shares Kant's skepticism as regards earthly happiness:

> No attained object of desire can give lasting satisfaction, but merely a fleeting gratification; it is like the alms thrown to the beggar, that keeps him alive to-day that his misery may be prolonged till the morrow. Therefore, so long as our consciousness is filled by our will, so long as we are given up to the throng of desires with their constant hopes and fears, so long as we are the subject of willing, we can never have lasting happiness nor peace.[4]

But, unlike Kant, Schopenhauer does not believe in a blessed eternal life in the hereafter. His subsequent pessimism is all the more radical in that, as the philosopher points out, when all our desires are satisfied, even in moderation, we become blasé! The pangs of desire make us suffer, but the calm of assuagement plunges us into boredom: "Thus [...] life swings like a pendulum backwards and forwards between pain and ennui."[5]

For Schopenhauer, happiness is an inaccessible goal and can be enjoyed, albeit imperfectly, only in creative activity, which is an endless source of novelty for the artist. Ultimately, it can be apprehended only negatively, he concludes: satisfaction and contentment are merely the cessation of a pain or a lack. With experience, says Schopenhauer, "we stop seeking happiness and pleasure and are solely preoccupied by escaping as much as possible from pain and suffering. [...] We see that the best we can find in the world is a present without suffering, one that we can peacefully tolerate."[6]

For many modern thinkers, this is where the definition of happiness ends: an instant's respite between two moments of suffering. This is the view of Freud, for example: "What we call happiness in the strictest sense comes from the (preferably sudden) satisfaction of needs which have been dammed up to a high degree, and it is from its nature only possible as an episodic phenomenon."[7]

Basically, the definition of happiness in Kant, Schopenhauer and Freud fits the way our ego works: the world has to yield to our desires. Hence its illusory character. But this definition gives short shrift to our mind's ability to leave this mode of operation and make us desire "what is." When our minds are thus enlightened, they lead our willpower to love life as it is, not as we would wish it to be. This is the extraordinary challenge of wisdom, both in the East and the West.

CHAPTER 19

The Smile of the Buddha and Epictetus

It isn't the things themselves that disturb people, but the judgements that they form about them.[1]

—Epictetus

It isn't things that bind you, but your attachment to things.[2]

—Tilopa

Both in India and in Greece, many sages claim to have found a way out of the dead end in which we find ourselves when we seek to adapt the world to our desires: turning the problem the other way round, sages seek to adapt their desires to the world. They aim to master them, limit them and even neutralize them so as to find an accommodation with the real. They may thus be satisfied with their lives, whatever the external factors that may come along and pose a potential threat. In other words, the happiness of the sages no longer stems from the always random events that come from a world outside them (health, wealth, honors, recognition and so on) but from the harmony of their inner world. It is because they have found peace within themselves that they are happy.

Rather than attempting to change the world, sages focus on changing themselves. Their happiness is immanent: it is realized here and now, in the world as it is, in one's innermost depths.

By turning things the other way round, happiness becomes possible. What poses an obstacle to happiness isn't reality but the way we represent it to ourselves. The same reality may be perceived differently by two people: one may derive happiness from it, the other unhappiness. A given individual may perceive a serious illness as a terrible blow of fate, while another, apart from the present pain, will see it as an opportunity for asking questions about life, changing this or that factor without losing their inner peace. When faced with aggression, some people will feel hatred and a desire for vengeance, while others will feel no resentment: "How many wicked people would I kill? Their number is infinite, like space. Whereas, if I kill the spirit of hatred, all my enemies are killed at the same time," writes the Buddhist sage Shantideva in *The Guide to the Bodhisattva's Way of Life*. And the Stoic sage Epictetus says something similar: "Remember that what insults you isn't the person who abuses you or hits you, but your judgement that such people are insulting you. So whenever anyone irritates you, recognize that it is your opinion that has irritated you."[3]

In fact, I have always been struck by the many resemblances between Buddhism and Stoicism. But more recently, I have also been intrigued by the similarities between the more flexible, human-scale forms of wisdom found in Montaigne or the Taoist sages Lao Tzu and Chuang Tzu, or the joyous non-dualism of Spinoza and the *Advaita Vedanta* of India as lived in a period closer to us by, for example, the sage Anandamayi Ma.

So it is these three great paths to wisdom—the transmutation of desire, an adaptable way of going along with
one's life and a joyful self-liberation—that can be found
in the East as well as the West, that I would like to describe in the next three chapters, as a way of responding
to the pessimism of the moderns. How can we reach the
deep happiness that is promised by wisdom? The first
way, proposed by Buddhism and Stoicism, is probably the
most radical: it aims to attack the source of the problem
by proposing to eliminate the thirst, the attachment.

Stoic wisdom was born in Athens in a context of political and religious crisis that is not without its similarities
to the one we are currently experiencing. Destabilized
by the conquests of Alexander the Great, the Greek city-
states had lost their sense of superiority over the rest of
the world, and were also being questioned by a powerful
surge of critical reason that led to traditional powers losing their authority. The need was felt for a new religious
language more in harmony with the advance of reason,
and this led to the emergence of schools of wisdom which
either set anthropomorphic gods aside (Epicurus), or replaced them by the figure of a single God accessible to
reason (Aristotle), or by an immanent and pantheist conception that identified the divine with the cosmos. This
latter vision was put forward by the Stoics.

The name of this new school came from the Greek
word *stoa*, the porch under which their founder, Zeno of
Citium (c. 335–c. 264 BC), taught. Zeno, a simple trader
from Cyprus, thus became the "Stoic," the "man of the
porch." Breaking away from the aristocratic tenor of
the teaching of Plato and Aristotle, and going back to

the figure of Socrates, Zeno aimed to bring philosophy out into the streets. Despised by the intellectual elites for not being Greek, he rapidly gained a hearing among the common people thanks to his forceful way of speaking and his very simple way of life. Addressing everyone—citizens, slaves, men and women, Greeks and immigrants, cultivated people and the illiterate—he founded a school that would have a huge influence over the whole of the Greek and Roman world for over seven centuries.

The bases of Stoic doctrine were written down by Zeno's main disciple Chrysippus in the middle of the third century BC. What are its guiding principles?

The first major idea is that the world is *one* (everything is simultaneously matter and spirit, as well as divine) and can be conceived as a great living body that follows the same natural laws and is peopled with correspondences (these days, we would say "connections"). The second idea is that the world is rational: the divine *logos* (reason) underlies it all, and all human beings are, through their personal *logos*, part of the universal *logos*. The third idea is that there is an immutable law of necessity or universal causation, which fixes the destiny of all individuals. The fourth, finally, affirms that the world is good: everything that happens occurs for the best, with regard to all beings (given the extraordinary complexity of life and the cosmos), even if we are not aware of this and live with the sense that things appear to be imperfect. It follows, from such a conception of the world, that the happiness of human beings resides in accepting what is, in cleaving to the cosmic order.

Epictetus lived in Rome in the first century AD. With Seneca and Marcus Aurelius, he was without a doubt one of the best popularizers of Stoic wisdom, but also the model of the accomplished sage, and was venerated as such in his own lifetime by a host of disciples. He had been a slave before becoming a philosopher, he was lame and poorly dressed, lived in a hovel and taught detachment to men and women of all conditions of life. Exiled from Italy at the age of forty by an edict of Domitian, who disliked philosophers, he took refuge in Nicopolis and founded a school there. Like Socrates, Jesus and the Buddha, he decided to write nothing himself. But his disciple Arrian summed up his teaching in the *Discourses*, which he further condensed in a short *Handbook*, which expresses the quintessence of Stoic philosophy: we should master ourselves and put up with adversity by distinguishing between what depends on us, what we can act upon and the rest, which we have no control over.

Epictetus gives two striking examples to help us understand his philosophy more clearly. First he describes a cart to which a dog is tied. If the dog resists, it will still be forced to follow the cart, pulled along by a strong horse, and will suffer terribly if it attempts to prevent the inevitable. But if it accepts the situation, it will go along with the movement and speed of the cart and will reach its destination safe and sound, with neither fatigue nor pain. The same applies to human beings: We need to unite our wills with the necessity of destiny. We have no say in what does not depend on us (our bodies, external goods, honors and so on), but we are able to acquiesce in the real world as it is and to change what does depend on us: opinions, desires and aversions. To clarify his ideas, Epictetus also uses the image of an actor: actors do not choose their roles—beggars or nobles, sick or healthy people, etc.— nor the length of the play, but they are entirely free in the way they perform their part: they can play well or badly;

perform with pleasure if the role suits them, or with reluctance or disgust if they don't like their parts. "Don't seek that all that comes about should come about as you wish, but wish that everything that comes about should come about just as it does, and then you will have a calm and happy life," concludes the philosopher.[4] He cites several other examples of the attitude we should take when we are thwarted or bothered by external events:

> With regard to everything that happens to you, remember to look inside yourself and see what capacity you have to deal with it. If you catch sight of a beautiful boy or woman, you'll find that you have self-control to enable you to deal with that; if hard work lies in store for you, you'll find endurance; if vilification, you'll find forbearance. And if you get into the habit of following this course, you won't get swept away by your impressions.[5]

Stoic wisdom states that desire affects the soul and forces it to yield: it is a "passion" of the soul. Instead of desire, the Stoics advocate will, moved by reason (*logos*); this can transform our blind desires into deliberate, self-aware movements. Instinctive desire, entirely focused on pleasure, is banished in favor of the lucid and rational will that leads to happiness, since will, conceived in this way, produces exclusively virtuous acts and eliminates the desires that can disturb the soul's tranquility. So Stoicism is a philosophy of *willpower*, requiring perfect self-control. Properly speaking, in fact, the Stoics do not claim to annihilate desires, but to convert them into will subjected to reason.

The two goals which Stoic wisdom aims for are tranquillity of soul (*ataraxia*) and inner freedom (*autarkeia*). This latter, as we have seen, consists of making our will coincide with the cosmic order: I am free when I will whatever happens by necessity. So I no longer complain, no longer struggle, no longer feel any resentment, but instead take joy in everything and, in all circumstances, preserve my inner peace.

In order to achieve this, the Stoics deployed remarkable psychological subtlety in analyzing the very many different human passions: they counted seventy-six of these, divided into thirty-one desires (including six forms of anger), twenty-six sorrows, thirteen fears and six pleasures. But in particular, they practiced spiritual exercises. The most well-known of these is vigilance (*prosoche*): an attention to each instant that enables us to adopt the appropriate attitude whenever an external event or an inner emotion arises. "Living the present" is one of the main precepts of Stoic practice, which teaches us to avoid any flight into the past, any escape into the future, to drive away all fear as well as all hope, to concentrate on the moment, where everything is tolerable and transformable, rather than allowing ourselves to be submerged by the fears, anxieties, angers, sorrows or desires aroused by our imagination.

Another important exercise, which seems somewhat to contradict the previous one, consists in anticipating disagreeable events—the *praemeditatio futurorum malorum*, as Cicero called it. This involves imagining some unpleasant event that might occur so as to "de-dramatize" the situation in advance by reflecting on it and preparing ourselves to have the most appropriate attitude if said event does actually occur.

Thus, the Stoics advocate a daily examination of conscience, mainly so that we can measure the progress we make each day, and meditation, which is essentially viewed as a "rumination," a memorization of the doctrine, so that we won't be taken by surprise when some disturbance occurs or our path is hampered by some episode. This is why later Stoicism—roughly speaking, that of Imperial Rome—rather dropped any interest in the school's theoretical foundations, focusing instead on the *practical advice* that would help us live: disciples would continually repeat this advice to each other. Thus, Roman Stoicism comprises a host of manuals, thoughts, discourses, letters and maxims that propose brief and striking sayings designed to help beginners persevere in their quest. These texts—including the *Handbook* and *Discourses* of Epictetus, the *Letters* of Cicero and Seneca, and the *Thoughts* of Marcus Aurelius—have enjoyed an exceptional popularity since then, as they can be understood and used in a different theoretical framework from that proposed by Stoicism itself. From the Fathers of the Church to Schopenhauer, via Montaigne, Descartes and Spinoza, the Stoic maxims have continued to fertilize Christian doctrine and the western philosophical tradition.

However, a few centuries before the birth of Stoicism, there appeared in India another form of wisdom that would promote almost the same ideas, namely Buddhism. Before we investigate the striking resemblances between these two great streams of wisdom, let's take a look at the foundations of Buddhism and ask how the question of happiness arises for it.

Siddhartha Gautama lived in the sixth century BC. His father was the head of a modest clan from north India, and Siddhartha enjoyed a sheltered childhood. He married, had a son, and at around the age of thirty encountered four different people who turned his life upside down. He met a sick man, an old man, a dead man and an ascetic. He suddenly realized that pain was the common lot of mankind and that nobody, rich or poor, could escape it. So he left his father's palace, abandoned his family and set off in search of a spiritual path that would enable him to escape this condition of suffering. After wandering through the forests for five years and devoting himself to extreme ascetic practices, he sat at the foot of a Peepal tree and entered a deep stage of meditation. It was then, according to Buddhist tradition, that he achieved Awakening: a complete understanding of the nature of things and a state of inner liberation. He then went to the Deer Park near Benares, where he found five of his former ascetic companions, and delivered his teaching to them in the long and celebrated "Discourse on the Setting in Motion of the Wheel of the Dharma," which contains the essence of his doctrine.

This doctrine is contained in four lapidary sentences (the Four Noble Truths) based on the world *dhukka* which is often translated as "suffering," though this should not be understood as any temporary pain, but as an enduring unhappiness linked to the inner fragility that makes us subject and vulnerable to all disagreeable external events: illness, poverty, old age and death. So what does the Buddha say? Life is *dhukka*. The origin of *dhukka* is thirst, understood in the sense of desire/attachment. There is a way of suppressing this thirst, and *dhukka* with it; this is the Noble Eightfold Path, or the Eight Right Elements.

Each of these formulations, which comprise the common basis of the different schools of Buddhism, deserves some explanation.

The first truth emphasizes non-satisfaction in life. It's the symptom of the malady that the Buddha sets out in seven experiences: birth is suffering, old age is suffering, death is suffering, being united with what we do not love is suffering, being separated from what we love is suffering, not knowing what we desire is suffering and the five aggregates of attachment are suffering. In other words, suffering is ubiquitous. Recognizing the first principle of non-satisfaction means admitting that we cannot bend the world to our desires. This lucid, objective realization is a first step on the Path.

The second truth is a diagnosis of the cause of suffering: this, says the Buddha, is desire, thirst, avidity and attachment, all of which chain beings to *samsara*, the incessant round of deaths and rebirths which itself is subject to the universal law of causality that rules the cosmos, namely *karma* (each act produces an effect).

The third truth states that a cure is possible: in order to achieve the complete ablation of this thirst, human beings are able to renounce the tyranny of desire/attachment and free themselves from it.

The fourth truth tells us what this remedy actually is: the "Eightfold Path," which leads to the cessation of suffering, in other words to *nirvana* (a state of absolute happiness linked to the extinction of thirst and the understanding of the true nature of things). Its eight components are: right understanding, right thought, right speech, right action, right livelihood, right effort, right mindfulness and right concentration. These eight elements traditionally correspond to three disciplines: ethical behavior, mental discipline and wisdom. By reiterating the term *right*, the Buddha is defining what is called the "Middle Way." He is said to have started his first discourse with these words:

> A monk must avoid two extremes. Which? Attaching oneself to the pleasures of the senses, which is low, vulgar, earthly, and ignoble, and engenders bad consequences; and giving oneself over to mortifications, which is painful and ignoble, and engenders bad consequences. Avoiding these two extremes, oh monks, the Buddha has discovered the Middle Path which gives vision and knowledge and leads to peace, wisdom, awakening and *nirvana*.

To understand how human beings reach this ultimate wisdom, we need to grasp the fact that it's the self, in other words the principle that produces and accumulates *karma* (the law of causality of all our actions), that gets caught up in the wheel of *samsara* and that, one day, in this life or another, will perhaps manage to free itself from *samsara* so as to gain *nirvana*. The Buddha defined the self as an ever-changing combination of five aggregates in a state of constant flux, which he lists as follows: the aggregate of the body (or of matter), the aggregates of sensations, of perception, of the formations of the mind (emotions, impulses and desires) and finally of awareness. He took a different view from Hinduism, and rejected the existence of a permanent self, the *atman*—a sort of eastern equivalent of the soul—in which he saw nothing but a mental projection. Instead, he recommended the doctrine of *anatman*, of non-self.

The activity of our ego seizes on these aggregates and

gives us the illusion of a stable identity, a permanent self. Buddhist practice aims at freeing us from this illusion, "leaving behind the ego," and thereby breaking through to an understanding of the ultimate nature of mind: a luminous state of pure knowledge outside all conditioning, which the Buddhist tradition of the Mahayana (the Great Vehicle) calls "the Buddha nature."

So *samsara* is not an objective condition of reality: the world is not, in itself, suffering. But because of our ignorance, we are in *samsara*, in other words in an erroneous perception of reality, linked to the ego and attachment. Knowledge of the true nature of things frees the mind from the errors of perception and negative emotions. This liberation consists in gaining an awareness of our true nature, the Buddha nature that slumbers in us and that we need to realize.

By discovering through the experience of Awakening this true nature of mind, we cease to be moved by the ego and can thus reach a stable and permanent happiness, because the insatiable desire which produces suffering is linked to the functioning of the ego. The Buddhist tradition uses the Sanskrit word *sukha* to refer to happiness in the sense I mean here: the peace and profound harmony of the mind that has transformed itself and is no longer subject to the vicissitudes of life with its pleasant and unpleasant events.

Just as for the Stoics, it would be reductive to claim that Buddhism enjoins us to renounce all desire. The desire it proposes to abolish is that which is created by attachment (*tanha*, in Sanskrit), while it actually encourages the noble desire to improve ourselves, to progress in the path of compassion, the impulse towards the good (*chanda*, in Sanskrit).

The list of points that these two traditions of eastern and western wisdom have in common is a long one.[6] They both conclude that pain is linked to agitation, to a troubled mind, and put forward a path that leads to a true happiness, which, here too, is identified with a deep and joyful inner peace, serenity, a mind at rest. They invite individuals to transform themselves through inner knowledge and effort, to adopt a right ethical behavior that promotes a balanced life between the extremes. They put forward a very subtle analysis of emotions and feelings, and a host of spiritual exercises enabling people to control their passions, to develop the focus and control of their minds and to cease being the playthings of their imagination.

But the similarities between the two schools of thought do not solely involve human psychology and spiritual progress. They are just as striking when it comes to their philosophical understanding of the world. They both have a cyclical understanding of time: the universe constantly goes through cycles of birth, death and rebirth. They both insist on the movement and impermanence of all things (the Stoics drew on the doctrine of "becoming" in Heraclitus, for whom all things are flowing, and according to whom you can never step twice into the same river); they emphasize the unity of human beings with the world, and the presence of a cosmic (or, for the Stoics, divine) dimension in human life that constitutes its true nature—Buddha nature for the Buddhists, the *logos* for the Stoics. They believe that things happen out of necessity, thanks to a universal law of causality (*karma* or destiny). But they also declare that it is possible to obtain freedom by working on our minds and attaining the right way of seeing things. It's perhaps on this last point that we might detect the most notable difference between Stoics and Buddhists: the latter, as we have seen, deny that the self has any substance, while the Stoics maintain the idea of a permanent individual principle, even if this, the *logos*, is in the final analysis merely a fragment of the universal *logos* to which it will attach itself after the death of the individual.

In the West, Buddhism and Stoicism have both frequently been criticized for being schools of passivity, concentrated on individual change, but not enough on changing society. This is a superficial view that fails to recognize the decisive historical impact that these two philosophies have had on the destiny of the world. By refusing to draw a distinction between individuals in accordance with their family or clan groups, their social and religious affiliations, considering instead that all human beings may attain Awakening or *ataraxia* by working on themselves, they brought about an extraordinary revolution in values. For these philosophies, what is worthy of respect is not social rank, but virtue. What should be admired and imitated is not the monarch or the aristocrat, or even the priest, but the sage, which means all those who have managed to master themselves. They have shown that the individual was not merely a cog in a community, and, by insisting on the equal dignity of all human beings, all endowed with the same fundamental nature, they established the idea of a universal human being, beyond individual cultures, and gave the world a profoundly subversive social vision.

Buddhism quite logically rejected the caste system, which led to its being banned from India. As for Stoicism, by proclaiming the ontological equality of all human beings, who carry the same divine *logos*, it broke the aristocratic stranglehold of Greek thought and paved the way for egalitarianism and Christian, and later modern, universalism.

> If our intellectual part is common, the reason also, in respect of which we are rational beings, is common: if this is so, common also is the reason [*logos*] which commands us what to do, and what not to do; if this is so, there is a common law also; if this is so, we are fellow-citizens; if this is so, we are members of some political community; if this is so, the world is in a manner a state. For of what other common political community will any one say that the whole human race are members?[7]

Over two thousand years before the Universal Declaration of Human Rights, the Stoics invented cosmopolitanism, the idea that all human beings are citizens of the world, and have equal rights. As for Buddhism, it is certainly the form of eastern wisdom most inclined to confirm such a message, which is part of its own essence.

These close links between Buddhism and Stoicism, and their modernity, explain why these two great forms of wisdom still speak to us nearly two thousand five hundred years after their appearance. At the same time, they can be viewed as the best antidotes to our own period's narcissistic individualism: for while they exhort individuals to freedom and autonomy, this is not by satisfying all their desires, but, in a completely different way, through self-mastery and detachment. While we extol the freedom of desire, these philosophies teach us to free ourselves *from* desire. This is a salutary lesson, but this probably makes it the most difficult of all to learn. The Stoics were aware of the almost superhuman character of the wisdom to which they aspired, but they were still committed to pursuing it as a permanent norm of their actions.

CHAPTER 20

The Laughter of Montaigne and Chuang Tzu

The glorious masterpiece of man is to live to purpose.[1]

—Montaigne

Running around accusing others is not as good as laughing.[2]

—Chuang Tzu

The path proposed by Buddhism and Stoicism if we are to attain wisdom is an arduous one. Happiness, inner peace and serenity come from the suppression of desires or their conversion into a rational will, and this is no light task. It's also a path that can be a very long one: the Buddhist tradition explains that we need many lives before we can achieve Awakening! Since we don't really know what stage we have reached in this karmic journey, and do not inevitably feel summoned to base our whole lives on the need to acquire this ultimate wisdom, let's consider another path towards happiness that may seem more accessible to us. It's a path on a more human scale, one that gives the simple pleasures of life their value, though without abandoning the main principle of wisdom according to which human beings have to learn to adjust their desires to the world, rather than vice versa.

As we have already mentioned, this is the path of moderate desires, advocated by Aristotle and Epicurus. Pleasures are, in themselves, good, we simply need to regulate them through reason: then the Supreme Good, happiness, can be identified with a stable state of pleasure. A French writer and thinker of the sixteenth century, Michel de Montaigne, had a rather similar viewpoint: he set out a cheerful, modest path to wisdom, one that was in tune with everyone's nature, and was an astonishing echo of the Chinese Taoist sages, in particular Chuang Tzu, the main founder of philosophical Taoism with Lao Tzu.

This wisdom can be summed up in a few words: nothing is more precious than life, and in order to happy, we just need to learn to love life and enjoy it in the proper, adaptable way, in accordance with our own natures. Chuang Tzu and Montaigne have another trait in common: humor. These two skeptics mock the dogmatic, enjoy relating irreverent anecdotes, deride the complacent and are able to laugh at themselves and those like them.

Pierre Eyquem came from a family of Bordeaux merchants, and in 1519 he became lord of Montaigne, a chateau and grounds acquired by his grandfather. Here, in 1513, was born Michel, who was thus known as Michel de Montaigne. Pierre became mayor of Bordeaux when Michel was twenty-one years old. Blessed with a likeable and cheerful nature, the young man embarked on law studies and became a counselor in the *parlement* of Bordeaux where he met Étienne de la Boétie, his greatest friend, who died prematurely five years after they met. At the age of thirty-two, he married Françoise de la Chassaigne, who gave him six daughters, only one of whom survived: Léonore. On the death of his father, Michel became the owner and lord of Montaigne. At thirty-eight, he retired to his chateau to embark on the writing of his *Essays*, published nine years later, in 1580. That same year, he undertook a trip to Germany and Italy lasting fourteen months, from which he returned to become mayor of Bordeaux, a post to which he had been elected during his absence. Although he was reelected, he abandoned the position in 1585 to devote himself to the republication of his *Essays*, on which he worked until his death in 1592, at the age of fifty-nine.

This apparently peaceful life was in fact lived in a particularly violent and disturbed historical context, one of epidemics, famines and the French Wars of Religion, which all had a major impact on his thinking.

Montaigne had read most of the sages of antiquity, including the Stoics, whom he quotes frequently. However, as he more or less openly admits, he feels quite unable to follow this path, at least in its radical form. Likewise, he expresses his admiration for Socrates, but only to state that he would have had no hesitation in running away rather than obeying the unjust law that had sentenced him to death: "If those [laws] under which I live should shake a finger at me by way of menace, I would immediately go seek out others, let them be where they would."[3] For Montaigne, the sages are of course figures for us to admire, and we need their example to show us the ideal of wisdom, but they cannot be imitated by just anyone. His position on this subject, as on many others, continued to develop, as is shown by the evolution of his thought in the *Essays*, the only work he wrote, which condenses into three volumes his life and his reflections on himself, the world, society, human beings and animals, life and death. Written in the French of his period, he is not always easy to read, despite the wonderfully flavorsome language he uses. However, his work contains treasures of wisdom and humanity.

Montaigne's relationship to death provides us with an excellent example of the way his thinking evolved. Taking inspiration from a formula of Cicero's,[4] he titles chapter 19 of the first volume of the *Essays* "That to Study Philosophy is to Learn to Die," and gives us a perfect lesson in Stoic philosophy: unlike the common people, we should be constantly thinking of death, so that we may grow used to it and no longer fear it when it happens. But, at the end of his life, when he wrote chapter 12 of the third book, he confessed that, all in all, it seemed preferable to him to be like the peasants he observed and not think about death at all. In the final analysis, death is just the "end," the "extremity" of life, neither its "aim" nor its "object." In short, life is much too precious to think of anything except life itself.

Montaigne admired Christ as much as he did Socrates, but he also found the ideal promoted in the Gospels too lofty: he decided that he himself was quite unable to give up his life, or even his belongings, or to be permanently filled with compassion for others. He was in search of a wisdom within his reach, one that he could actually attain. "I am no philosopher; evils oppress me according to their weight."[5] He sought to avoid difficulties, useless polemics, tricky situations, complications. He endeavored not to think about things that bothered him, not to

ruminate over his worries, but to enjoy life's little pleasures and to think, as much as possible, only about the
things that made him cheerful.

This wisdom of everyday life was something that
Montaigne practiced in his personal as well as in his professional life. In politics, he deployed an art of compro-
mise, avoided confrontation and decided that his role
consisted more in finding the necessary accommodations
than in proposing great plans or attempting to revolu-
tionize the order of things. In his personal life, as in politics, one thing struck him as certain: it was best to avoid
the great passions, those that upset the mind, led one
into the illusion of the limitless and made one prone to
extreme actions.

If Montaigne thus advocated a modest and limited
path, this was because he was seeking a wisdom that
would fit him, one that was *in conformity with his nature*, with what he—Michel de Montaigne—actually was.
Here, we touch on what is probably the most original, but
also the most profound, aspect of his thinking. For what
he criticizes in the great schools of antiquity isn't just the
almost inaccessible character of their ideal, it's also the
systematic nature of their doctrine, which was supposed
to apply to everybody. But Montaigne was convinced that
we should all be able to find the path to happiness that
suits us, depending on what we are, our character, our
sensibility, our physical constitution, our strengths and
weaknesses, our dreams and aspirations. Montaigne's critique of the dogmatism of the great philosophical schools
was based on a profound skepticism inherited from the
Greeks, especially Pyrrhonism. It is in the "Apology for
Raimond Sebond," the longest and most highly structured of the *Essays*, that he sets out his doubts about the

ability of human reason to attain to universal truths, to be able to speak about God or to claim to decipher the riddles of nature.

He begins by mocking the human claim to arrogate a central place in nature, and states that nothing makes us superior to, or even different from, the animals except our pride: "It is not upon any true ground of reason, but by a foolish pride and vain opinion, that we prefer ourselves before other animals."[6] Those who know and are fond of animals will really enjoy reading the many pages Montaigne devotes to their sensitivity, their memory and their passions, as well as their intelligence, their goodness and their wisdom. He then attacks theoretical knowledge and science, and starts by noting that, when it comes to obtaining happiness, they are not of the slightest use: "I have known in my time a hundred artisans, a hundred labourers, wiser and more happy than the rectors of the university, and whom I had much rather have resembled."[7] Then he tries to demonstrate the basic inadequacy of human reason to apprehend God, the world, the true and the good. Montaigne states that he has faith and believes in God, but he's convinced that this faith can only be the fruit of a divine revelation in the heart of each individual. All that has been and will be said about God in the metaphysics of the philosophers or the scholasticism of the theologians is just empty words resulting from the projection of our human qualities and passions onto an "incomprehensible power."

The same applies to those philosophers who claim to decrypt the laws of nature: the world will always evade our understanding, and no philosophical system can ever explain its complexity and its harmony. Furthermore, if all the great thinkers are forever contradicting one another on God, the world, the good and the true, he notes, this is because these things are all inaccessible to human reason.

But does this mean we need to give up on thinking and philosophizing? No, for Montaigne refuses to become tied down, like Pyrrho, to an absolute skepticism. In his view, what is important is to seek a balance between dogmatism and skepticism. This has been brought out very eloquently by Marcel Conche in his essay, *Montaigne ou la conscience heureuse* (Montaigne or the happy consciousness):

> Like the skeptics, we should suspend our judgment about things themselves and abandon trying to express the being of anything at all. Like the dogmatics, we must try to judge, and to live the life of the intelligence. We won't be skeptical, for we will reach an opinion and we won't hesitate to proffer it; we won't be dogmatic, for we won't be claiming to express the truth, but simply what, for us, at a given moment, appears as the truth.[8]

So what Montaigne criticizes the philosophers for is not that they express their opinions, far from it: opinion is precious and is a stimulus to further thought. Where they go wrong is in tricking their ideas out as absolute truths. But we can think of the world, or God, only on the basis of our own selves and the contingencies of our lives. This is why the philosopher can never attain certainty, merely communicate *personal convictions*. In other words, a philosophy expresses first and foremost what is felt and thought by a human being in a given society and at a specific moment in history. People of a pessimistic temper will produce philosophies imbued with pessimism, just as optimists will be inclined to view mankind and the world through optimistic eyes.

What is phony is erecting our philosophy, our vision of human beings, the world or God into a universal system. Two centuries before Immanuel Kant, Montaigne put metaphysics to death. This helps us understand the objective he was pursuing in the writing of the *Essays*: expressing a living, flexible thinking that follows the ups and downs of everyday life, one that is subjective and far removed from any dogmatic pretention. In this respect, he is probably the first of the modern thinkers, as Nietzsche did not fail to see: "The fact that a man such as Montaigne wrote has truly increased the joy of living on earth."

Drawing inspiration from the famous confession of Socrates—"All that I know is that I know nothing"— Montaigne chose as his motto "*Que sçay-je?*" or "What do I know?" and as his emblem a pair of scales, a symbol of balance and of suspension of judgment. Noting that "everything has many faces and several aspects,"[9] he endeavors to see things from many different points of view, to shift his gaze, to place himself in the position of others. This is why he is so fond of observing, listening and traveling. His journeys and his encounters with individuals from very different cultures and milieus merely confirm his relativism: everything is perceived in terms of the point of view of the person who looks at or experiences it. Our values are good for us, but are they good for others? The same applies to entire ethnic groups.

Montaigne was profoundly shocked by the way the Indians of the New World were treated—not just by the violence with which they were conquered, but also by the condescending and contemptuous manner in which their way of life, their customs, their beliefs and their rites were considered. Although he was a Christian, Montaigne felt that religion was just the expression of a culture, like language or lifestyle:

> We only receive our religion after our own fashion, by our own hands, and no otherwise than as other religions are received. [...] Another religion, other witnesses, the like promises and threats, might, by the same way, imprint a quite contrary belief. We are Christians by the same title that we are Perigordians or Germans.[10]

Not content with emphasizing the relativity of values and religions, Montaigne goes even further and says of the Indians of the New World—of which he met, at court, a few poor specimens exhibited like strange beasts—that these "savages" who seemed to need civilizing would in fact be better suited to teaching *us* a few lessons. He was struck by their naturalness: while our customs have gradually taken us further and further away from nature, these men and women live as close to nature as is possible, they are simple, spontaneous, true, and, in the final analysis, happy. Montaigne launches out on a fierce but accurate comparison between European town-dwellers who are sated but perpetually dissatisfied and these "savages" who, living simply in accordance with their natural and necessary needs as described by Epicurus, are always cheerful. Speaking of the Brazilians, he notes that, for them, "the whole day is spent in dancing" and "they are, moreover, happy in

this, that they only covet so much as their natural neces-
sities require."[11]

It is precisely by comparing ourselves with these Indians, he says, that we can see how far, in spite of the
importance of our religion, our knowledge and our material comfort, we are "out of joint," unable to be happy in
accordance with the natural order. We constantly seek
our happiness by projecting ourselves onto the external,
material world, whereas it can be found only within us,
in the profound satisfaction that we can derive from the
simple pleasures of life, which generally cost nothing.

The important thing, given all this, is that we should
know ourselves, in the sense of knowing our own nature:
Montaigne is asking, *What is good for me?* His philosophy emerges from what he feels, what he sees, what he
discovers and experiences within himself. This is why his
philosophy suits him, but it's for the same reason that
it affects us: he is inviting us to do the same, to relearn
to think on the basis of our senses, our experiences, the
observation of ourselves, and not just on the basis of
theories we have learned (the thoughts of other people), the customs and prejudices of the society in which
we live.

This brings us to a crucial point in Montaigne's
thought: his conception of education. He lambasts the
way educators are always trying to stuff the heads of children with all kinds of knowledge that will be of very little
help in teaching them how to live well. The real educative
project should consist in teaching children to develop
their *judgment*. For the most essential thing in leading a
good life is to be able to discern and judge things well.
The formation of judgment is inseparable from self-
knowledge: an educator must teach children to come to

a judgment about things on the basis of themselves, their sensibility and their own experience.

This doesn't mean that we should give up the attempt to transmit to children values that are essential to a shared life, such as good faith, honesty, loyalty, respect for others and tolerance. But we should help children to gauge the importance of these virtues on the basis of their own feelings, their own ways of seeing. By teaching them to know themselves and observe the world with a spirit that is at once open and critical, we can help them to form a personal judgment which will enable them to make choices in life that suit their individual natures. In short, education must teach people to think well so as to live better—and, as we have seen, this is the main task of philosophy as the ancients understood it. Instead of a "well-filled" head, the educational objective of his time—and what does this imply about ours?—Montaigne prefers a "well-made" head; rather than the quantity of knowledge, he emphasizes the quality of judgment: "We only labour to stuff the memory, and leave the conscience and the understanding unfurnished and void."[12]

"A man should diffuse joy, but, as much as he can, smother grief."[14] Here we find, in a nutshell, Montaigne's program for life. This program has an apparent simplicity—the same simplicity to which our natures spontaneously incline us—but Montaigne emphasizes that it is actually followed by very few so-called "civilized" people, who instead tend to make their lives too complicated, creating difficulties either by a chaotic lifestyle in which they are the slaves of desires they can never assuage, or conversely by allowing a perverted moral and religious conscience to load onto them burdens that are too heavy to be borne.

In order to increase joy and diminish sadness, two conditions need to be met: we should learn to know ourselves, and also regulate our judgment so as to discern what is the best for ourselves, without thereby harming others. As a good Epicurean, Montaigne is intent on being as happy as possible (in accordance with his nature) while enjoying all the fine pleasures that life grants him every day: going horse riding, enjoying a tasty meal, meeting friends and so on. But he insists on two aforementioned points: the need to be aware of our happiness, to take time to appreciate it and enjoy it as intensely as possible; and the quality of attention that we need to bring to bear on each of our experiences: "When I dance, I dance; when I sleep, I sleep."[14]

Just as he savors the pleasures of experience, Montaigne endeavors as much as possible to avoid its pains. He shuns all avoidable suffering and seeks, as we have seen, the compromises that simplify social life and make it more pleasant, rather than stoking divisions and making problems even more toxic for the sake of great principles or political passions.

In his private life, he himself was sometimes forced to face tough challenges. Faced with health problems, he advocates a completely Stoic wisdom of acceptance, and— as he considers that illness is part of the natural order of things—he recommends that we allow the body to carry out its own repair work and avoid treating ourselves with any remedies other than those provided by nature. We should say that there was not a great deal to recommend the medical treatment available in his day: he lost five of his six children, "if not without grief, at least without repining,"[15] as he puts it without blinking, for even here he feels that these bereavements are part of the natural order of things, and there is no point in getting upset.

This is also why he condemns any idea of "sacrifice" and refuses to share the sufferings of others. There's too much suffering as it is, he says, for us to add our own to that of others. Help others, yes, but not at our own expense. Act with courage, but never exaggerate our strengths.

Montaigne's wisdom comes down to a sort of great, sacred "yes" to life. We should know and accept our own natures so that we can learn to enjoy life. We should shun any avoidable suffering and patiently put up with the inevitable trials of life while continuing to try and enjoy what gives us contentment. We should make up for the brevity of existence by the quality and intensity of our experiences. This is the only way we can confront death without regret.

> Chiefly that I perceive [my life] to be so short in time, I desire to extend it in weight; I will stop the promptitude of its flight by the promptitude of my grasp; and by the vigour of using it compensate the speed of its running away. In proportion as the possession of life is more short, I must make it so much deeper and fuller. [...] For my part then, I love life and cultivate it, such as it has pleased God to bestow it upon us.[16]

Around two thousand years earlier, a philosophical trend emerged and developed in China that has astonishing similarities with the thought of Montaigne: Taoism. This trend began with two men and two short works: Lao Tzu, considered as the author of the *Tao Te Ching*, and Chuang Tzu, the author of a book which bears his name.[17]

According to the legend, Lao Tzu lived around the sixth and fifth centuries BC, which would have made him a contemporary of Confucius. He was an archivist at the court of the Chu kingdom and left this country as a result of political disturbances. As he crossed the border, it is said that Han Kou, the guard of the pass, asked him to leave something in writing. Thereupon he composed the *Tao*, commonly translated as *The Way and Its Virtue*. Comprising eighty-one brief chapters in rhyme, this is a book of great profundity and poetic flavor, and is indisputably one of the great texts in world literature. Most current historians, however, emphasize the fact that Lao Tzu's historical existence is unattested and that the work was probably composed a few centuries later, by several authors.

On the other hand, the existence of Chuang Tzu, who lived at the end of the fourth century BC, is almost certain. The book attributed to him, and bearing his name, belongs to a very different literary genre, which allows its author's personality to emerge: ironic, skeptical, facetious, libertarian. His—more substantial—work is woven out of tales, anecdotes, parables, little stories and piquant dialogues, all of a rare philosophical profundity. In its form, it already makes us think inevitably of Montaigne's *Essays*, even if it is probable that the work was filled out in subsequent centuries by his followers.

Chuang Tzu was born in the southern kingdom of Chu, and seems, like Montaigne, to have occupied an administrative post before retiring from the world in order to write. Indeed, both men show a great mistrust towards those who aim to change the world through political action. Their skepticism and their cyclical conception of history lead them instead to the conclusion that it's more important to know and transform ourselves than to try and transform the world and society. The *Book of Chuang Tzu* contains an anecdote that speaks volumes about the kind of person he was.

> Once, when Chuang Tzu was fishing in the P'u River, the king of Ch'u sent two officials to go and announce to him: "I would like to trouble you with the administration of my realm."
>
> Chuang Tzu held on to the fishing pole and, without turning his head, said, "I have heard that there is a sacred tortoise in Ch'u that has been dead for three thousand years. The king keeps it wrapped in cloth and boxed, and stores it in the ancestral temple. Now would this tortoise rather be dead and have its bones left behind and honored? Or would it rather be alive and dragging its tail in the mud?"
>
> "It would rather be alive and dragging its tail in the mud," said the two officials.
>
> Chuang Tzu said, "Go away! I'll drag my tail in the mud!"[18]

Another significant similarity with Montaigne is this: Taoism emerged at a time of violent political struggle, the period of the Warring States, which preceded the unification of the Chinese Empire in 221 BC (and this Empire lasted until 1911!). So it was in this time of troubles that the first great Chinese thinkers tried to find an answer to a deep social and political crisis. While Confucius proposed a ritual path that respected tradition, encouraging political commitment with the aim of creating virtuous people and a virtuous society, Lao Tzu and Chuang Tzu advocated a completely different path: we should withdraw from the affairs of the world, and aim for individual improvement guided by the observation of nature, following our own essence.

Admittedly, the Confucian sages also proposed nature as a model of wisdom, but they did not view it from the same angle as the Taoists: they promoted a human wisdom closely based on the perfect and immutable order of Heaven, with the emperor as the center and the supreme model on earth. As for the Taoists, they looked at the living, mobile, diverse and apparently chaotic nature of the earth, and put forward a wisdom of fluidity, flexibility, movement and spontaneity, which aimed to be at harmony not with an immutable cosmic order, but with the very abundance of life. While Confucius wished to develop civilization by establishing a stable moral order, this was precisely what he was criticized for by Lao Tzu and, particularly, Chuang Tzu, who—like Montaigne—advocated the idea that human beings should be freed from the artifices of culture and custom, faithful to the spontaneity of their own nature, listening to their deep and singular being and aspiring to live in profound harmony with an inexplicable and ever-changing nature.

Before we examine the main features of Taoist wisdom, let's say a few more words about its philosophical and cosmological underpinnings. The word "Tao" is quite close to the Buddhist concept of *dharma* and means "path," "way." But it also refers to the fundamental principle, the source, the origin, the root, of the world. It's the

Tao which regulates the universe and maintains cosmic harmony. The Tao is indefinable and cannot be understood. No word, no notion can contain it. As Lao Tzu poetically puts it:

> Look at it but you cannot see it!
> Its name is *Formless*.
> Listen to it but you cannot hear it!
> Its name is *Soundless*.
> Grasp it but you cannot get it!
> Its name is *Incorporeal*.
> These three attributes are unfathomable;
> Therefore they fuse into one.[19]

The Tao also explicitly involves an idea of flowing, of flux, and refers to the way nature is constantly changing. Its tangible face is the *Taiji*, the universe as we perceive it, a great living organism ruled by a universal law of causality. Everything is interdependent, every creature is a fragment of this living cosmos and is linked to all other beings. Chinese medicine rests on this conception of a world in which macrocosm and microcosm correspond to one another.

Two opposite forces crisscross this permanent flux of cosmic life: *yin* and *yang*. Yang expresses the active masculine dimension that springs forth, separates, organizes and conquers. Yin expresses the passive feminine principle that gathers, unites, dilutes and pacifies. Yang is light, the emergence of life, fire, sun and day. Yin is shadow, disappearance/transformation of life, cold, moon and night. They should not be viewed as two antagonistic forces, but as two complementary and inseparable poles. They express themselves as a process: all life is manifested and flows dynamically through this dialectic of yin and yang.

Unlike Confucian intellectualism, Taoism rejects any possibility of forming a system of knowledge: its philosophy is imbued with skepticism. Chuang Tzu is the great "deconstructor": before Montaigne, he casts derision on those philosophical schools that claim to tell us what is true while simply engaging in ever more protracted dialogues of the deaf. He rejects any idea of an unambiguous truth and constantly emphasizes the need to break away from binary logic, that of the excluded middle (a thing is either true *or* false, it is either this *or* that). For him, on the contrary, a thing may be this *and* that. This is why, far from being demonstrative, his arguments are circular; he always proceeds by shifting his point of view and looking at things from many different and contradictory angles. So he loves to express his thought through the mouths of marginal figures, drunkards, unsophisticated and "unreasonable" people, who are able to state deeper and more paradoxical truths than those put forward by intellectuals.

But, as Montaigne will later do, he can also make a definite statement, come to a conclusion and give his own point of view. Instead of dogmatic certainties, he prefers to give us his intimate convictions, while knowing that they are always provisional and questionable. He doesn't say: "I know nothing" but: "Do I know anything?"

The skepticism of Chuang Tzu comes across, for example, in his deconstruction of language: words can express only very imperfectly the depth, the ever-moving, ever-swarming richness of reality and life. Words freeze reality by adopting one culturally defined point of view, and so we need to mistrust them, relativize them, and even laugh at them. With this aim in mind, Chuang Tzu invents apparently absurd expressions and stories that are meant to destabilize reason and logic. In this respect, and several centuries before the introduction of Buddhism into China and Japan, he was the real precursor of the celebrated *koan* of Zen Buddhism.

If we are to avoid being trapped in the conventional usage of language and the intellectual and cultural postures that go with it—a belief in action, an emphasis on willpower, the belief that human beings occupy a supreme place in nature—we need to come back to observation, the senses, experience, and we need to settle down and humbly listen to life, to the "secret melody" of the universe that links us to the world through the heart and intuition. Hence Chuang Tzu's interest in craftsmen who perform their job with precision and efficiency without needing to think about it: the hand does what the intellect cannot say. He gives us the example of a butcher who tells how he managed, thanks to many years of experience, to cut up an ox with incredible dexterity without even blunting the edge of his knife. This training, which consists in carefully locating the way the animal's limbs are put together, has enabled him to acquire a skill without resorting to words or concepts.[20] This should be true of each and every one of us: we should learn to live not by learning things in some theoretical way, but through a life experience, through a training of body and mind that will give us practical wisdom. Here too, we can see that Chuang Tzu prefigures Montaigne in his educational principles, insisting on our need to rediscover naturalness, spontaneity, the vital impulse—all the things that are most important, but that education and custom tend to stifle.

This brings us to the heart of the teaching of the Taoist
sages: the doctrine of non-acting. Whereas we are taught
to transform the world and act upon it through the force
of our willpower, Lao Tzu and Chuang Tzu advocate
a wisdom of gathering in, being receptive, abandoning
control—a wisdom of fluidity and non-willing.

> Does anyone want to take the world and do what
>   he wants with it?
> I don't see how he can succeed.
> The world is a sacred vessel, which must not be
>   tampered with or grabbed after.
> To tamper with it is to spoil it, and to grasp it is
>   to lose it.[21]
> [...]
> Tao never makes any ado,
> And yet it does everything.[22]

This is not a matter of passivity but of letting-go.
These precepts are not advocating fatalism but rather
observation, patience, flexibility of reaction and action.
We should not "force" things, but go along with them.
Chuang Tzu often uses the example of swimmers, who
don't progress by imposing their will on the wave or the
current, but go along with its flow: "I go under with the
swirls and come out with the eddies, following along
the way the water goes and never thinking about myself.
That's how I can stay afloat."[23]

This allegory reminds me of the one Montaigne uses:
he talks of the horseman who goes along with the movement of his mount. Antoine Compagnon eloquently sum-
marizes it thus: "One image expresses his relation to
the world: that of horse riding, the horse on which the
horseman keeps his balance, his precarious seating. My

'seating' (*assiette*)—that's the word he uses. The world moves and I move: it's up to me to find my seating in the world."[24] Chuang Tzu loved to swim, but there's no doubt that, if he'd been a horseman, he'd have used the same image as Montaigne, as it is the best way of expressing the relation we need to have to the permanent movement of the world. He is also trying to show that it is intellectual prejudices and all the expressions of our ego—fear, apprehension, the desire to succeed, comparison—that make us unhappy and stop our lives from flowing freely along. Once these screens have been removed, we can adjust ourselves, naturally and aptly, to the flow of life and the world.

To promote this philosophy of "non-acting," Lao Tzu and Chuang Tzu counter the dominant social values and state that the weak can overpower the strong. Lao Tzu expresses this idea by using the metaphor of water:

> Nothing in the world is softer and weaker than water;
> But, for attacking the hard and strong, there is nothing like it!
> For nothing can take its place.
> That the weak overcomes the strong, and the soft overcomes the hard,
> This is something known by all, but practiced by none.
> Therefore, the Sage says:
> To receive the dirt of a country is to be the lord of its soil-shrines.
> To bear the calamities of a country is to be the prince of the world.
> Indeed, Truth sounds like its opposite![25]

Another frequently used image is that of the child, completely unable to act and yet able, by its mere presence, to get adults moving. The child is the center of the family, and acts without acting. Thus the sage shouldn't take a mature person as a model, as Confucius had advocated, but rather the little child, as Lao Tzu writes:

And be the Brook of the World.
To be the Brook of the World is
To move constantly in the path of Virtue,
Without swerving from it,
And to return again to infancy.[26]

Chuang Tzu gives us a little story in which Nan-Po asks Niu-Yu why, in spite of his great age, the latter had kept the complexion of a small child. The answer, says Niu-Yu, is that he has heard the Tao.

The wisdom of "non-acting" leads to *detachment*, in other words to a profound acceptance of life and its laws: birth, growth, decline and death. If sages do not fear death, this is because they consider it to be part of the natural rhythms of life. So, when faced with the death of their near ones and dear ones, they show a detachment that may well shock those around them.

The *Book of Chuang Tzu* relates this story:

Chuang Tzu's wife died. When Hui Tzu went to convey his condolences, he found Chuang Tzu sitting with his legs sprawled out, pounding on a tub and singing. "You lived with her, she brought up your children and grew old," said Hui Tzu. "It should be enough simply not to weep at her death. But pounding on a tub and singing—this is going too far, isn't it?"

Chuang Tzu said, "You're wrong. When she first died, do you think I didn't grieve like anyone else? But I looked back to the beginning and the time before she was born. Not only the time before she was born, but the time before she had a body. Not only the time before she had a body, but the time before she had a spirit. In the midst of the jumble of wonder and mystery a change took place and she had a spirit. Another change and she had a body. Another change and she was born. Now there's been another change and she's dead. It is just like the progression of the four seasons, spring, summer, autumn, winter.

Now she's going to lie down peacefully in a vast room. If I were to follow after her bawling and sobbing, it would show that I don't understand anything about fate. So I stopped.[27]

Here again, one can't help thinking of Montaigne. Both thinkers teach us a profound acceptance of life as it is and not as we would like it to be if we could control it. So it comes as no surprise to discover, in both Chuang Tzu and Montaigne, the deep sense of joy that infuses those who have learned to love life and greet it with open hearts. Taoist sages are full of joy, they live in the here and now, without brooding over the past or worrying about the future, in the full acceptance of the enjoyment of the present moment. Their joy comes from non-action, from the way they have managed to melt into the flow of the Tao and of life to fulfill themselves in profound harmony with nature. The sage "sees clearly into what has no falsehood and does not shift with things," as the *Book of Chuang Tzu* puts it. "He takes it as fate that things should change, and he holds fast to the source. [...] A man like this doesn't know what his ears or eyes should approve— he lets his mind play in the harmony of virtue. As for things, he sees them as one and does not see their loss."[28]

The joy of the sages comes from the fact that they have renounced everything that might separate them from the breath and the harmony of the Tao. It is by renouncing their egos that they become fully themselves, fully human. Such are the paradoxes of Taoist wisdom: it is by forgetting ourselves that we find ourselves, by refusing to act that we have influence, by becoming little children that we attain wisdom, by accepting our weakness that we become strong, by looking to the Earth that we discover Heaven, by fully loving life that we can serenely accept death.

How, one last time, can we fail to think here of Montaigne? In him, as in Chuang Tzu, we find a love of life and a joyful acceptance of fate based on a deep religious sense. It hardly matters that Montaigne talks of God but Chuang Tzu of the Tao. Although Marcel Conche is himself an atheist, he has written about Montaigne in terms that apply equally well to Chuang Tzu and are an eloquent expression of the ultimate root of the joyous happiness of those two skeptics, both of them so sensitive to life's sacred dimension:

> It is not for us to look towards that which dispenses weal and woe. It would be indiscreet to try and catch the giver in the act of giving. Let's lower our eyes. The absolute sun from which all radiance comes is not meant to be seen by us. Let

us be content with the radiance without trying to scrutinize its source. The true way of looking towards God is to look towards the world and welcome it as a gift. [...] Consenting to enjoyment is true humility. The act of enjoyment is the real thanksgiving if it is accompanied by humility and gratitude. It is the most religious of acts, an act of communion with the unfathomable, inscrutable but tirelessly generous power that is both nature and nature's source. We need to enjoy religiously, in other words while respecting what is enjoyed, with fervor, a serious attentiveness and an awareness of mystery.[29]

And with a great burst of laughter!

CHAPTER 21

The Joy of Spinoza and Ma Anandamayi

Joy is a man's passage from a lesser to a greater
perfection.[1]

—Baruch Spinoza

On July 27, 1656, there took place, in the synagogue of
Amsterdam, a ceremony of unusual violence: the elders
uttered a *herem*, a solemn act of banishment, on a young
man of twenty-three, accused of heresy:

> With the judgment of the angels and of the saints
> we excommunicate, cut off, curse, and anathema-
> tize Baruch de Espinoza. [...] Cursed be he by day
> and cursed be he by night. Cursed be he in sleep-
> ing and cursed be he in waking, cursed in going
> out and cursed in coming in. The Lord shall not
> pardon him, the wrath and fury of the Lord shall
> henceforth be kindled against this man, and shall
> lay upon him all the curses which are written in
> the book of the law. The Lord shall destroy his
> name under the sun.[2]

Not only was the young Baruch Spinoza not actually overwhelmed by any curse from heaven, but his name still shines today in the firmament of mankind. "All philosophers have two philosophies: their own, and Spinoza's," as Bergson was to put it three centuries later. The fact remains that this terrible punishment was the equivalent of a banishment for the young son of a Portuguese merchant whose family had already had to flee the Inquisition to find refuge in Amsterdam, in a small Calvinist republic that tolerated the presence of a sizeable Jewish community. The young Bento, whose name had been Judaized into "Baruch," changed his first name yet again upon his exclusion: he adopted the Christian name of "Benedictus." However, he did not convert to Christianity, even though he admired Christ, and most of his friends were Christians who were open to the "new ideas" of Descartes, Galileo and Locke then turning upside down the old world that had been based on the truth of the Bible and Thomistic scholasticism. He now turned to the Latin language to compose a philosophical work focused on blessedness, supreme happiness. After all, don't his three successive first names all mean "blessed"?

Spinoza pursued his quest for happiness through a very sober lifestyle. Not only did he renounce his inheritance from his father: he also refused to inherit anything from his wealthy friends, accepting just a modest income that complemented what he earned as a lens maker. It's a piquant thought that the man who tried as much as possible to sharpen the discernment of the mind chose a profession that consisted in improving our visual faculties! In addition, Spinoza decided not to have a family and lived out his life surrounded by friends and disciples, in rented rooms in various towns in Holland. In a single room, sometimes two small rooms, were his books, his writing desk, his optical workshop and the only object to which he was attached: the four-poster bed in which he was conceived, in which he would die and in which he slept after his parents' death. This bed was doubtless a symbol of continuity within a turbulent and continually threatened life. His books were, even when published anonymously, banned by the censors. And yet everyone knew that he was the author of the notorious *Tractatus theologico-politicus* that carried out a radical, rationalistic deconstruction of the Bible and advocated the creation of a secular state that would guarantee freedom of religious and political expression. In spite of the threats that menaced him (including an attempt at assassination), Spinoza was surreptitiously read and admired by the whole of intellectual Europe. He turned down offers from several prestigious universities, and even an invitation from Louis XIV to teach in Paris where he would have drawn on a comfortable income. He knew that, if he accepted, he would lose his liberty of thought and preferred to carry out his modest activity as a lens polisher for the rest of his life.

His health was fragile and he struggled to finish his magnum opus, the *Ethics*, a veritable treatise on happiness, which aimed at nothing less than procuring salvation, in other words blessedness and supreme liberty, in this world, through the efforts of reason alone. Shortly before dying, he asked a friend to get a barrel of beer for him, and some conserve of roses, for his convalescence—which shows that his choice of a sober life did not entail total asceticism, as some people have thought. Probably suffering from tuberculosis, he died in his room, alone, on February 21, 1677, at the age of forty-four. His doctor, a friend, arrived shortly after, leaving with his precious manuscripts. In this way, the *Ethics* was published six months later, thanks to an anonymous donation, in a volume of *Posthumous Works* that was immediately censored.

In the *Ethics*, the first part is dedicated to the question of God; the second to the question of the mind; the third to the affects; the fourth discusses the bondage produced by the emotions; and the fifth is about freedom and blessedness. At first, one might wonder why the religious and political authorities felt they had so much to fear from such a work. Furthermore, the work is difficult and demanding to read: written drily, built up in a geometrical style—with definitions, axioms, propositions, demonstrations, scholia and corollaries. However, behind this aridity and the heavy feel of a closed metaphysical system that Montaigne would have rejected with scorn (everything is logically linked together on the basis of definitions and axioms that need to be accepted), an attentive reading of the work reveals a set of ideas that are both enlightening and revolutionary. Encountering Spinoza can change your life.

The question has often been raised of why Spinoza constructed his *Ethics* in a geometrical mode. It may be a tendency of his era—one to which Descartes also succumbed, giving an appearance of scientific rigor to metaphysical ideas—but it can also be seen as a style produced by persecution, as Leo Strauss has shown. There is evidence for this in the Latin motto and seal chosen by Spinoza: *Caute*, be careful! Without necessarily sharing the scathing irony of Jean-François Revel, for whom "in this external cladding there is hardly any more necessity than in a game where a treatise of gastronomy is presented in the form of a penal code,"[3] we might indeed conclude that Spinoza would have chosen another form of utterance if he'd been writing in a regime where there was complete freedom of expression.

There's another problem that we should point out: Spinoza uses the same metaphysical vocabulary of his time—substance, mode, attribute, essence, existence, soul, etc.—that we find in Descartes, Leibniz and Malebranche, but he sometimes gives the words he uses a new meaning. The same goes for the word *God*, which he identifies with nature, thereby making a profound break with the western metaphysical tradition. This makes him an "atheist" in the strict sense of the term, as we shall see later.

Let's return to the question of happiness, which is our main concern and also the principal aim of his *Ethics*: his whole system, which begins by defining God-Nature, then focuses on defining the human being so as to establish an ethical wisdom, in other words a rational path that aims to lead human beings to blessedness and complete freedom.

One of the most modern aspects of Spinoza's thought— one that has attracted the attention of several biologists and neurologists—is the central place occupied by what he calls the "affects," which we would these days designate as emotions, feelings and desires. Spinoza is an extraordinary observer of human nature. The way he describes every affect and its interrelations with the others is amazingly relevant: joy, sadness, love, anger, envy, ambition, pride, mercy, fear, hatred, contempt, generosity, hope, anxiety, the over- and under-rating of the self, contentment, indignation, humility, repentance, melancholy

and so on. Long before Schopenhauer and Freud, he realized that human beings are essentially driven by their
affects.

At a time when emphasis was placed on the knowledge of the soul and the spectrum of virtues and vices
in attaining spiritual fulfillment, Spinoza shows that the
journey towards liberty and happiness begins, rather,
with an in-depth exploration of our desires and emotions. If he insists so much on this question, this is, he
explains, in order to free us from a cruel illusion: that of
free will. Not that Spinoza rejects any idea of freedom,
but freedom (unlike the awareness we have of it) does
not reside in our will, which is always influenced by an
external cause. Human beings are subject to a universal
law of causality (here we find a fundamental concept
common to both Buddhism and Stoicism), and cannot be
freed from their inner servitude without the aid of reason,
after a long process of active self-knowledge that enables
them to cease being unconsciously driven by their affects
and by inadequate ideas. Human beings are not born free,
they become free: the *Ethics* aims to provide them with
a method for achieving that joyous freedom that Spinoza
considers to be a veritable *salvation*, a liberation: "Man's
lack of power to moderate and restrain the affects I call
bondage. For the man who is subject to affects is under the control, not of himself, but of fortune, in whose
power he so greatly is that often, though he sees the better
for himself, he is still forced to follow the worst."[4]

So we need to understand the chain of causes and
effects that conditions our thoughts, our desires and
our feelings. With this aim in view, Spinoza studies human beings as animals subject to the universal laws of
nature and severely criticizes those who, like Descartes,

"conceive man in Nature as a dominion within a dominion."[5] Avoiding all preconceived ideas about any supposed "specificity" of human being—and here, he is close to Montaigne—Spinoza sets out to show that all living beings must be studied and distinguished in terms of the affects of which they are capable (this is exactly the same project that we find in today's ethology). To this end, Spinoza frees himself from Christian and Cartesian dualism, which radically separates soul from body by viewing the soul, considered as immortal, to be preeminent over the body. For him, while we can draw an abstract distinction between soul and body, the two are inseparable in concrete life and function in parallel, without one being superior to the other. The word "soul" (*anima*), with its freight of theology and metaphysics, is indeed used only rarely by Spinoza, who prefers the word "mind" (*mens*). Unlike Descartes, he doesn't view body and mind as two different substances, but as one single and identical reality expressed in two different *modes*: the body is a mode of extension while the mind is a mode of thought.[6]

Once he has clarified this point, Spinoza shows that: "Each thing, as far as it can by its own power, strives to persevere in its being."[7] This effort (*conatus* in Latin) is a universal law of life—something that modern biology would confirm: "the living organism is constructed so as to maintain the coherence of its structures and functions against numerous life-threatening odds," as the famous neurologist Antonio Damasio, a fervent reader of Spinoza, puts it.[8]

Just as naturally, as Spinoza again insists, each organism constantly endeavors to attain a greater perfection, an increase of its power. But it is forever encountering external bodies that it affects or that affect it. When this encounter, when this "affection" increases its power of acting, a feeling of joy is the result. Conversely, the change to a lesser perfection, and the lessening of the power of acting, arouse a feeling of sadness.

Joy and sadness are the two affects, the two main feelings of every sensitive being. And they are completely dependent on the external causes that produce them. Spinoza uses these two affects to explain the other feelings: love, for example, is defined as "joy with the accompanying idea of an external cause,"[9] in other words the affect of joy reflects back onto the idea from which it stems just as, conversely, hatred is born of the idea from which the feeling of sadness stems. People who love endeavor to have present, and to conserve, the thing or person that they love, just as those who hate endeavor to remove and destroy the thing or person to which they are averse.

All of our affects, notes Spinoza, are the products of our own nature, of our being and our specific power of acting. The encounter with a certain person or a certain thing can be profitable or harmful to both, or profitable to the one and harmful to the other. What counts is discerning what suits *us*, what increases our power to act and thus our joy, and conversely what diminishes it and produces sadness of whatever form.

Montaigne would have been thrilled at this, too! For Spinoza, there's nothing more absurd than the idea of universal rules of action or behavior (apart from the laws that govern communal life, of course). We must all learn to know ourselves in order to discover what makes us happy or unhappy, what is appropriate or not, what increases our joy and lessens our sadness. Spinoza uses the metaphor of poison to get across the idea that everything happens at a basically biological stage: there are bodies, things, people who poison our organism, just as there are others that contribute to its growth and flourishing. If we are prepared to swallow poison, this is because our minds are polluted by all sorts of inadequate and erroneous ideas that lead us to believe—under the influence of certain affects of our imagination or of an external morality—that what is poisoning us is in fact good for us. Hence the need to attain to a true knowledge of *what we are* if we are to know what suits us, but also the need the abandon the attempt to follow an external code of morals, one that is dogmatic, transcendent and claims to be valid for all.

Long before Nietzsche—and this is one of the many reasons for the latter's profound admiration for the Dutch philosopher—Spinoza put forward an amoral vision of the world, beyond Good and Evil. He replaced the religious and metaphysical categories of Good and Evil with the categories of what is good and evil *for us*: "We call good, or evil, what is useful to, or harmful to, preserving our being."[10] What is good, for us, is when a foreign body harmonizes properly with ours and increases its power, and thus our joy. What is bad (rather than "evil" as such) is when a body inappropriate to ours poisons us, intoxicates us, makes us ill, diminishes our power to act and thus produces sadness in us.

In a first sense, the good and the bad thus comprise relative descriptions of what suits or does not suit our natures. But in a broader sense, Spinoza calls "good" a reasonable and firm mode of existence that endeavors to organize our life in tune with what makes us grow, suits our nature, makes us happier and more joyful, and "bad" a disordered mode of existence, senseless and weak, which makes us unite with things or persons that go against our nature, lessen our power and eventually plunge us into sadness and unhappiness.

Outside the *Ethics*,[11] Spinoza gives an original reading of the "fault" of Adam, who fell after eating the fruit of the Tree in spite of the divine warning. What Adam takes as a moral prohibition is in fact merely a divine piece of advice aimed at guarding him against the temptation of eating a fruit that will poison him because it is not in conformity with his nature. Adam's fault, for Spinoza, lies not in the fact that he disobeyed God, but that he did not follow a judicious piece of advice and thus made himself ill by eating the fruit. As Gilles Deleuze points out in his enlightening work on Spinoza,[12] this critique of transcendental morality is also a critique of conscience, which, failing to perceive the correct logical chain of causes and effects, feels the need to establish an inexplicable external order: the transcendental and irrational morality of "thou shalt," of "one must," then replaces the immanent, perfectly rational ethics of the knowledge of what is good and bad. We can find comfort and indeed encouragement in attributing the moral rules which we respect to an inexplicable external order. The transcendent morality of "thou shalt" enables us to avoid thinking about what we know to be good or bad for us.

This means that a passion is no longer denounced as a sin or a vice, as happens in Christian theology or classical morality, but as a form of slavery, a *servitude*. Yet again, the whole project of the *Ethics* is aimed at freeing human beings from their inner servitude thanks to knowledge.

Nevertheless, Spinozism is not a philosophy exempt from *laws* valid for all, in other words, rules inherent in the respect for others and common life. Far from it: throughout his work, Spinoza insists on the necessity of a just law, to which all citizens must submit, which condemns all physical or moral violence inflicted on individuals. But what he aims to show in the *Ethics* is that this common and necessary law, born of reason, is not in the least opposed to a personal pursuit of individual happiness that is also the fruit of reason, and must lead all of us to discover, through our own efforts, what is good and bad for each one of us. Spinoza is convinced that the individual discovery of what is useful to us and what makes us happy is also useful for the happiness of all and the quality of the lives we lead together. "When each man most seeks his own advantage for himself, then men are most useful to one another."[13]

In other words, self-knowledge is the most precious of gifts when it comes to living together, as it means that individuals no longer have to live under the blind sway of their passions, the source of all violence. Even if Spinoza does not say so, it is self-evident that if all individuals lived under the sway of reason and could attain complete self-knowledge, they would be so perfectly responsible that there would no longer be any need for any external law to ensure that order prevails in the life of the community.

In this long itinerary of liberation through knowledge, Spinoza draws a distinction between three "kinds" of knowledge, three ways of knowing. Opinion and imagination comprise the first kind, the one that keeps us in our state of servitude. The second kind is universal reason, which enables us to discern, distinguish, know and order our affects. Intuition, thanks to which we can grasp the relation between a finite thing and an infinite thing, is the third kind; through it, we can become aware of the adequate fit between our inner world, ordered by reason, and the totality of Being, between our intimate cosmos and the whole Cosmos, between ourselves and God. This intuitive grasp gives us the greatest felicity, the most perfect joy, since it enables us to be in harmony with the whole universe.

Let's make one essential point clear: Spinoza was aware that reason alone is not enough to undertake this long, demanding path of liberation. For this it needs a motive force, a source of energy. He sees *desire* as the motor that leads human beings to hoist themselves from an imperfect joy to an increasingly perfect joy. "Desire is the very essence of man,"[14] he writes. And, rather than attempting to annihilate desire or stifling it by the force of will—as do the Buddhists, the Stoics and Descartes—he thinks it is better to use it, to regulate it, to turn it towards an ever more adequate and proper aim. Spinoza explains that "*desire* can be defined as *appetite together with consciousness of the appetite*"[15] (our appetite, our impulse, our need, becomes conscious) and explains that "we desire nothing because we judge it to be good, but on the contrary, we call it good because we desire it."[16] The best means of struggling against a bad desire is thus to put it in competition with a more powerful desire. The role of reason then consists not in judging and reprimanding a bad desire (as morality does), but in arousing new desires, more securely established, that will bring us greater joy.

Let's take a concrete example. I've got a twenty-three-year-old niece, Audrey, who didn't entirely thrive in her school studies—which bored her—and turned to a more vocational sales course, even though she was intellectually bright. Once she'd become a saleswoman, she grew even more bored and told herself that she'd be unhappy if she continued to do this job all her life long. Impelled by her curiosity and an appetite for knowledge, she spontaneously decided to start reading general interest books; she discovered an interest in sociology, which seemed more suited to her desire to gain a better understanding of the world in which we live. By dint of personal hard work, she managed to get a place in university and is currently making a great success of her studies, which make her happy. Without any of her family or friends forcing her to do so or wagging a finger at her, Audrey has realized that her nature needed to acquire knowledge if it was to blossom, and she replaced one desire (making a living from sales) by another that was more appropriate to her (understanding the society we live in). Reason helped give her a justification and basis for this new desire and enabled her to do all that was necessary to make a success of it, including the financing of her studies. This is a simple example, but it's a good illustration of this aspect of Spinozist philosophy. At the opposite pole from any imperative morality of duty, Spinoza founds an ethics of desire based on attraction.

He points out, too, that: "An affect cannot be restrained or taken away except by an affect opposite to, and stronger than, the affect to be restrained." [17] What this means is that reason and will are not enough to suppress an emotion or a feeling that disturb us. Their role lies in fostering the emergence of a more powerful emotion or feeling than those which cause us sadness, and that will alone be able to eliminate the cause(s) of our sadness. Spinoza tells us that happiness depends not just on our vigilance in eliminating disturbing thoughts and emotions, but also on the way we manage to develop positive thoughts and emotions. It's not enough to knuckle down to eliminating obstacles and poisons if we are to be happy, we also need to focus on energizing the forces of life: to nourish joy, love, compassion, kindness, tolerance, benevolent thoughts, self-esteem, etc., as we have been discussing. This is the basis of the contemporary trend in positive psychology which insists on the need not to concentrate solely on our problems, our disturbed emotions, but also and above all to become aware of our life potential and to develop everything that might be able to help us, by our own resources, to overcome our wounds and our inhibitions. The best way of fighting against fear is to develop confidence. And the best way of fighting against hatred is to develop its opposite: compassion.

Tibetan Buddhism, the Buddhist tradition which has investigated the transformation of the emotions in the greatest depth, jibes with this view and offers us a veritable "alchemy of the emotions": spiritual exercises that aim at developing the opposite emotion from the one that is bothering us. This is what happens in so-called *tonglen* meditation, which involves visualizing a person or situation that are a source of anger, fear or resentment. When breathing in, we visualize black smoke emanating from these negative persons or "objects," which we then absorb, and when breathing out we project a white shining light on these "objects" or persons. This helps us move gradually from a negative to a positive emotion, from anger to benevolent love, from anguish in the face of a situation to a state of serenity.

The same applies to ideas: we cannot suppress a false—or rather, in Spinoza's precise language, an "inadequate"—idea by just rejecting it, but by comparing it with an "adequate" idea, in other words refuting it by a superior argument that, as if by a force of attraction, will lead reason to support it. In this way, for Spinoza, the philosophical journey will be a path leading from an imperfect understanding to a correct grasp of things, from disordered desires to good desires, from limited joys to the perfect joy which he calls *blessedness*. In the meantime, all progress, every new stage, every step forward comes with a new and greater joy, since it increases our power of being. From joy to joy, human beings can thus travel towards blessedness and the higher freedom in which our being coincides with that of God—"*or* Nature,"[18] as Spinoza adds.

And it's on this final point that I'd like to conclude this brief summary of the *Ethics*. If we take atheism to be the negation of a personal, creative God as revealed by the Bible, then Spinoza is clearly an atheist, as he denies the existence of such a God, one that has been produced by "the imagination of theologians." But this doesn't mean his philosophy can be described as "materialist"—even though this often happens—since by identifying "infinite substance," which he calls God, with nature, he is not thereby reducing it to matter. For him, mind and matter, like mind and body, are one, made of the same substance. Thus, Spinoza is at once both a spiritualist and a materialist. Or he is neither ...

So we can claim that his thought is imbued with religious feeling not because he observes the dogmas of this or that religion but because, like the Stoics, he puts forward the vision of a cosmos subject to a law of necessity emanating from the first Substance (God), which alone is acausal, and a path to salvation which finds its end, as in Aristotle, in divine contemplation: "This, then, is the sum

of our supreme good and blessedness, to wit, the knowledge and love of God."[19]

Spinoza always rejected the claim that he was an
atheist, or anti-religious. We will not follow him on the
first point here, as his atheism is clearly proven, even if
he had to deny it out of political prudence. But we can
understand how, without being religious, he was not anti-
religious. The philosophical path that he puts forward
leads, like religion, to salvation and blessedness, but by
following an enlightened reason and desire. This path,
which he himself viewed as "very hard,"[20] was one that
he recommends to philosophers, in other words to those
who endeavor to emerge from servitude through rational
wisdom. But he absolutely does not despise those (and
there are countless more of them) who hope to reach
salvation through faith and the practice of their religion.
Indeed, he states that the two aims converge and that the
teaching of the Prophets leads by other paths to the practical conclusions of the wisdom he is proposing.

If the "joy" of the saints and mystics proceeds from
faith and not reason, the fact remains that this joy is also
the result of a blessedness that emerges from their union
with God. The blessedness of which Spinoza speaks in
the *Ethics* appears to him to be more perfect, and above
all more stable and enduring, since it is the result not of
a subjective faith with its subjective hue, but of an objective reason pushed to the limit of its possibilities. Mystics
believe in God (and imagine this God to be a personal
being) and draw their joy from union with God, while the
wise *know* God (a God whom they have discovered to be
infinite Substance) and have realized God in themselves:
"Whatever is, is in God, and nothing can be or be conceived without God."[21]

• • •

Anybody with even a cursory understanding of Hindu philosophy cannot fail to be struck by the extraordinary kinship between Spinozist metaphysics and the metaphysics of India, particularly that which stems from the tradition known as *Advaita Vedanta*, or non-duality. Unlike the dualist tradition, which—exactly as in the case of the three great monotheist religions, Judaism, Christianity and Islam—draws a distinction between, on the one side, a transcendent, creator God and, on the other, a world created by that God, the non-dualist tradition postulates that there is a unity between God and this world. God does not exist outside the world; the world and God are part of the same substance; everything is in God, and God is in everything. Based on certain *Upanishads* (ancient texts more or less contemporary with the Buddha), the path of non-duality was particularly developed by one great Indian philosopher of the eighth century AD: Shankara. The core of his doctrine lies in the identification between the impersonal divine *brahman* and the individual self of *atman*. *Atman* is the *brahman* in human beings, and the whole aim of wisdom consists in realizing that there is no substantial difference between *brahman* and *atman*.[22]

Like Spinoza, Shankara did not despise the dualist religious paths that were so countless in India: resting on faith and love, they enabled millions of the faithful to experience a spirituality that was attainable by all, by adoring a deity or its avatar (that is, its manifestation or its incarnation). But he also says that the non-dualist path is a more profound expression of reality: the realization of being, the ultimate aim of all human life, implies the cessation of all duality. It is because they have escaped duality that sages become "liberated while

still alive" (*jivan mukta*), for whom there is nothing left
other than the "complete felicity of the pure consciousness, which is One" (*saccidananda*). Thus, deliverance is
the result of a coming to awareness both intellectual and
intuitive (*prajna*), which closely resembles Spinoza's third
type of knowledge, and which brings supreme happiness,
unbounded joy. However, there is one major difference
between Spinozism and *Advaita Vedanta*: while Spinoza
rejects the existence of an immortal soul, the Indian
doctrine affirms the existence of an immortal self (*atman*) which transmigrates from one existence to another,
from one body to another (vegetable, animal or human)
and aspires to escaping the cycle of *samsara* (the endless
round of rebirths) to attain deliverance (*moksha*) by realizing its identity with *brahman*. This is, from a certain
point of view, a considerable difference, since in the one
case individual consciousness ceases on the death of the
body, and in the other it does not: but the difference isn't
all that crucial for those who embark on the path of wisdom and, in this life, achieve the intuitive understanding
that enables them to identify their being with that of the
whole Cosmos. From this arises the supreme joy, which
is "pure felicity" for Hindus and "eternal blessedness" for
Spinoza: "We feel and know by experience that we are
eternal."[23] Eternal, not immortal: but it hardly matters,
for Spinoza, what happens to us after death, since we can
at every instant experience eternity, experience the divine
substance with which we are identical, and which is a
source of infinite joy.

In his work *Le Bonheur avec Spinoza* (Happiness with
Spinoza),[24] the philosopher Bruno Giuliani suggests an

interesting parallel between the thought of Spinoza and
the teachings of a great contemporary Hindu sage, Ma
Anandamayi, who died in 1982: she wrote nothing, but her
oral teaching has been transcribed by her disciples. Here
is an extract that could indeed have come from Spinoza:

> How can we escape this dilemma, this swing of
> the pendulum between happiness and unhappi-
> ness? You let yourself go amid the little joys of
> everyday life, but you don't bother to discover
> the source of them, the supreme Blessedness,
> from which all happiness stems. How much lon-
> ger will you continue to go round in circles? Can
> you hope to enjoy all the pleasures of the world
> and at the same time gain access to the supreme
> source of joy? [...] What you need to understand
> is that true joy exists only in the spiritual life. The
> only way to experience it is to know and under-
> stand what the universe truly is. We need to set
> our minds aright if we are to see that the whole
> world is divine. Our old world must disappear.
> Instead, we must see the world as it is, see God
> in all things, in all shapes and under every name.
> There isn't an inch of earth where God is not. The
> only thing we have to do is to open our eyes and
> see Him in good, in evil, in happiness and unhap-
> piness, in joy and sadness, and even in death. The
> words Life and God are interchangeable. If we
> become aware that all life is the One, we will be
> granted a changeless bliss.[25]

The name of this Hindu woman, a perfect contemporary representative of the Indian tradition of non-duality,

was not unknown to me, far from it. I must have been fifteen or sixteen when I had a strange experience. I was walking through Paris, in the rue de Médicis, opposite the Luxembourg Gardens, when my eyes were drawn to the window of a bookshop. For a long time I was unable to turn my gaze away from the cover of a book, which had the photo of a contemporary Indian sage by the name of Ma Anandamayi on it. Without my being able to explain why, her face, radiant with joy, overwhelmed me. She seemed to embody the absolute bliss of those "liberated while still alive," those who have perfectly realized their selves, according to the doctrine of *Advaita Vedanta*, and are now one with the universe, with God. I couldn't meet Spinoza, see his joy radiating, but I could meet this woman. And so, aged just twenty, when I decided to spend several months in India in 1982, I determined to go to one of the several ashrams she had founded. Unfortunately, I never managed to meet her, since she was dying and passed away during my stay in Benares.

Later on, I met one of her main French disciples, the journalist Arnaud Desjardins, who said of her:

> My personal life has given me the good fortune to gaze on many marvels, but what made far and away the strongest impression on me [...] was meeting a human being, a Hindu woman of Bengali birth, the famous Ma Anandamayi. This unforgettable, decisive experience has been shared by a huge number of Hindus and Westerners. Even the best images in a film and the most successful photos can communicate only a small part of her radiance. All the facets of an accomplished human being, from the bright laugh of a

child to the immense gravity of a sage, were expressed in her.[26]

He gave me a few photos of her, and I have to say that I often look at them and derive joy from them. Reading Spinoza fills me with joy, like the radiance of Ma Anandamayi, who expresses the realization of wisdom.

As I was finishing this chapter, I found myself, by a lucky coincidence, asked to give a lecture at The Hague, the last city in which Spinoza lived. I took this opportunity to fulfill a long-postponed dream: to visit the cottage in Rijnsburg, in the suburbs of The Hague, where Spinoza lived between 1660 and 1663, and which is now a small museum. I was overwhelmed to be going into the room where he started writing the *Ethics*, and where his library has almost entirely been reconstituted! The Nazi ideologue Alfred Rosenberg, fascinated by Spinoza, had confiscated this library and transported it to Germany without discovering that two Jewish women were hiding in the attic of the house.

I was just about to leave the museum when the guard, who had kindly agreed to stay there for an extra hour as I'd arrived just a few minutes before closing time, asked if I would write my name in an impressive register, and pointed to the name of Albert Einstein, who spent a whole day in the philosopher's room, on November 2, 1920, as the register attests. I knew that Einstein was a fervent admirer of Spinoza, and had declared in April 1929, to Herbert Goldstein, the prominent New York rabbi, who asked whether he believed in God: "I believe in Spinoza's

God who reveals Himself in the orderly harmony of what exists, not in a God who concerns himself with the fates and actions of human beings."[27] I then discovered that he also composed a poem dedicated to Spinoza on his visit to Rijnsburg: the poem hangs on the wall in a little frame and begins with this stanza:

> How I love this man
> More than I can say in words.
> And yet I fear that he will remain alone
> With his shining halo.

This phrase resounds inside me, echoing the last sentence of the *Ethics*, which I cannot fail to remember: "All things excellent are as difficult as they are rare."[28]

Epilogue

I'm happy and there's no reason for it.[1]
—Christian Bobin

Once upon a time, there was an old man sitting at the gate to a city. A stranger came up and asked him:

"I've never been to this city—what are the people who live here like?"

The old man answered with a question of his own:

"What were the people like in the city you've come from?"

"Selfish and wicked. In fact, that's why I left," said the stranger.

The old man replied:

"You'll find the same kind of people here."

A little later, another stranger came up and asked the old man: "I've just arrived, tell me what the people who live in this city are like."

The old man replied:

"Tell me, my friend, what were the people like in the city you've come from?"

"They were kind and welcoming. I had many friends. It wasn't easy for me to leave them."

"You'll find the same kind of people here," replied the old man.

A merchant who was watering his camels not far from there had heard both conversations. No sooner had the second stranger gone away than he asked the old man, reproachfully: "How can you give two completely different answers to the same question?"

"Because everybody carries their world in their heart."

This short Sufi tale is an eloquent expression of what, in their many different ways—as we've seen throughout this book—the sages of the whole world tell us: in the final analysis, happiness and unhappiness are within us. An unhappy person will be unhappy everywhere, those who have found happiness within themselves will be happy everywhere, whatever conditions they are living in. Kant, Schopenhauer and Freud are all pessimists who claim that a complete and enduring happiness is impossible because of the infinite character of human desire: to this, the sages of both East and West reply that this happiness *is* possible on condition that we no longer strive to adjust the world to our desires. Wisdom teaches us to desire and love what is. It teaches us to say "yes" to life. A deep and permanent happiness becomes possible once we have transformed the way we look at the world. We then discover that happiness and unhappiness don't depend on external causes, but on our "state of mind."

I began this work with a sociological definition of happiness: to be happy is to love the life we are leading. If, at the end of this work, I had to give a personal definition of happiness, I'd say that it is quite simply "love of life." Not just the life we are leading here and now, which can indeed provide us with many satisfactions, but life as such—life that, tomorrow, may well give us joy or sadness, pleasant or unpleasant events. Being happy means loving life, all of life: with its ups and downs, its glimmers of light and its periods of darkness, its pleasures and its pains. It means loving all the seasons of life: the innocence of childhood and the fragility of old age; the dreams and turbulence of adolescence; the fulfillment and the creaking joints of maturity. It means loving birth and also loving death. It means living through sorrows whole-heartedly and without reserve, and enjoying, just as fully, all the good times that are given to us. It means loving our friends and family with open and generous hearts. It means living each moment intensely.

We shouldn't confuse suffering with unhappiness. However paradoxical it may appear at first, we can simultaneously suffer and be happy. Suffering is inevitable, unhappiness is not. We can be enduringly happy even while experiencing suffering, and, so long as this suffering is temporary, it doesn't necessarily make us unhappy. It is universal, not immutable. We all experience it, and this doesn't make us all happy. While pleasure can't be associated with a state of suffering (apart from masochists!), we can be happy even when we're ill, or in a transient state of emotional or professional difficulty. This doesn't mean that we should do nothing to eliminate it—quite the opposite: when faced with suffering, we need to avoid any fatalism and seek to suppress its cause as much as we possibly can. But if there's nothing we can do about it, if we are powerless in the face of an illness, one of life's trials or some injustice, we can still act on our inner selves so that these problems do not have an adverse effect on our serenity.

What counts is never being crushed by pain and never allowing ourselves to relapse into unhappiness.

Unhappiness comes from the perception we have of suffering: one and the same pain may make us unhappy or not. The feeling of unhappiness is a product of our minds. Several different individuals may well have to undergo the same trials but they won't all be necessarily unhappy—and if they are, it will be to different degrees.

The mind can give meaning to suffering, can transmute it, set it within a wider set of perceptions. A woman can simultaneously suffer physically from the pains of giving birth and yet be filled with happiness at the idea of bringing her child into the world: she integrates the physical pain into the wider perspective of her child's birth. Much more radically, the Christian martyrs of antiquity went joyfully to their deaths, convinced that, in return, they would be given eternal happiness in the presence of a God whom they cherished more than anything.

And so the sense of happiness and unhappiness comes, in the end, from the mind. For those who have not yet experienced this, such a statement gains in persuasiveness because it is uttered not just by professional thinkers or sages from long-ago antiquity, but by ordinary people, our contemporaries, who say it on the basis of experiences they have lived through. I refer the reader to the work of my friend Alexandre Jollien, who spent seventeen years in a specialized institute because of a grave physical handicap that he was born with. In his books, Jollien expresses his joy, in spite of the times of suffering and doubt through which he went. There are many other such overwhelming accounts, and I'd like to quote one in particular.

Etty Hillesum was a young Jewish Dutch woman, deported to Auschwitz where she died at the age of twenty-nine. In the diary she kept for the two years leading up to her arrest, a time when she knew she had little chance of evading deportation, she wrote:

> When you have an interior life, it doesn't matter which side of the prison fence you're on. [...] I have already died a thousand deaths in a thousand concentration camps. I know about everything and am no longer appalled by the latest reports. In one way or another I know it all. And yet I find life beautiful and meaningful. From minute to minute.[2]

A few weeks before she was deported, she found herself in the transit camp at Westerbork, from where she sent her friends letters describing the appalling conditions. But her love of life never left her:

> The few big things that matter in life are what we have to keep in mind; the rest can be quietly abandoned. And you can find those few big things anywhere, you have to keep rediscovering them in yourself so that you can be renewed. And in spite of everything you always end up with the same conviction: life is good after all. [...] The realms of the soul and the spirit are so spacious and unending that this little bit of physical discomfort and suffering really doesn't matter all that much. I do not feel I have been robbed of my freedom; essentially no one can do me any harm at all.[3]

These words may remind us of the "inner citadel" of the Stoic sages and the ultimate freedom referred to by Spinoza, which has nothing to do with freedom of choice, of movement or of expression (Etty Hillesum enjoyed none of these forms of freedom), but which is the outward form of an inner joy that nothing and nobody can take from us.

Following Freud, Pascal Bruckner states that wisdom is these days impossible:

> There is not for us, there will probably never again be, any wisdom in the face of suffering, of the kind the ancients put forward, and as the Buddhists still offer, for the simple reason that wisdom presupposes a balance between the individual and the world and this balance has been long since broken, at least since the beginning of the Industrial Revolution.[4]

Etty Hillesum and Alexandre Jollien, among others, are a stinging disproof of this assertion. Human beings possess minds, and for this reason they are—and always will be—able, whatever upheavals the world may undergo, to attain wisdom. They won't necessarily be able to change the world, but they will always be able to change their way of perceiving it and to draw a changeless joy from this labor of inner transmutation.

Yet again, it has to be said that you can't bring happiness into being by decree, and it sometimes comes along without being sought for. But it can also be the fruit of everyday attentiveness, of vigilance, of an inner process. What the Greek philosophers called *askesis* is, in the etymological sense of the word, an "exercise," a training of the mind. Following the Greek and Buddhist sages, as well as Spinoza, we can seek to free ourselves from the "servitude" of our affects through patient work on ourselves. We can also, following Chuang Tzu and Montaigne, seek to live the right way, flexible and detached, taking pleasure in the joy of being, without necessarily following that ultimate form of wisdom. We can place all our ethics in the service of attaining supreme happiness or living better lives, but this has meaning only because happiness and life are desirable. As Robert Misrahi puts it, "ethics is the philosophical enterprise of rebuilding life from the viewpoint of joy."[5] I would add that we are all called upon to philosophize, in other words to think more correctly and live as much as possible in accordance with our thinking.

Joy can be viewed in two ways: as an intense emotion—the joy of passing our exams, watching our football team win, meeting up with a close friend and so on—or else as a permanent feeling in which our deepest being is immersed. This joy is not just a passing emotion, it's our essential truth. We feel it when we are in accord with ourselves, with others and with the universe. It is the result of the radiance of happiness or love, which is why it is often confused with happiness and love: the joy of living, a sense of gratitude, a sense of harmony within us and between the world and us. It isn't an extra, as if something external were being grafted onto us. It results from a process of unveiling: it preexists in us, and it is our task to bring it out. This involves clearing the path: we need to remove the obstacles that block access to this indestructible peace and freedom that lie within us.

So the exercise of the mind consists of eliminating whatever within us lies in the way of the joy of living. But what we actually do is the complete opposite: we try to be happier by eliminating *external* obstacles. We strive to improve our material comfort, to be more successful in our professional lives, to gain more recognition from our peers, to be surrounded by people who will provide us with pleasures. We focus all our efforts on external life and neglect working on ourselves, gaining self-knowledge, mastering our impulses, eliminating disturbing emotions or erroneous mental representations. But, though we need not neglect our outer lives, inner labor is indispensable for those who aspire to a more stable and deeper happiness, who wish to live better lives. Philosophical knowledge, understood as a spiritual exercise, enables us to liberate the joy buried in our hearts. Like the sun that never stops shining above the clouds, love, joy and peace are always there in our depths. The Greek word *eudaimon* (happy) makes this clear: *eu* (in accordance) *daimon* (genius, divinity); to be happy, for the Greeks, meant above all living in accordance with our good genius or with the element of the divine within us. I would say: vibrating in harmony with our deepest being.

Notes

Prologue

1. Epicurus, "Letter to Menoeceus," available online at www
.epicurus.net/en/menoeceus.html (accessed June 30, 2014).
2. Aristotle, *Nicomachean Ethics*, translated by W. D. Ross
(Kitchener, Ontario: Batoche Books, 1999), book 1, section 9
(p. 14), available online at socserv2.socsci.mcmaster.ca/econ
/ugcm/3ll3/aristotle/Ethics.pdf (accessed June 30, 2014).
3. Sigmund Freud, *Civilization and Its Discontents*, translated
by James Strachey (New York: W. W. Norton & Co., 1962),
pp. 30–31.
4. Epicurus, "Vatican Sayings," no. 27, available online at www
.epicurus.net/en/vatican.html (accessed June 30, 2014).
5. Pierre Hadot, *Philosophy as a Way of Life: Spiritual Exercises from Socrates to Foucault*, edited with an introduction
by Arnold I. Davidson, translated by Michael Chase (Oxford:
Blackwell, 1995), p. 104.
6. Ibid., pp. 104–105.
7. Robert Misrahi, *Le Bonheur. Essai sur la joie* (Paris: Éditions
Cécile Defaut, 2011), p. 25.
8. Louis Antoine de Saint-Just, in a speech to the National Convention, March 3, 1794.
9. Gustave Flaubert, *The Letters of Gustave Flaubert, 1830–
1857*, translated by Francis Steegmuller, volume 1 (Cambridge,
Mass.: Belknap, 1980), p. 62.

10. Freud, *Civilization and Its Discontents*, p. 23.
11. André Comte-Sponville, *Le Bonheur désespérément* (Paris: Librio, 2009), p. 11.
12. Pascal Bruckner, *L'Euphorie perpétuelle. Essai sur le devoir de bonheur* (Paris: Grasset, 2000; Le Livre de poche, 2002), p. 19.

Chapter 1: Loving the Life You Lead

1. Jean Giono, *La Chasse au Bonheur* (Paris: Gallimard, 1991).
2. Michel de Montaigne, *Essays*, book 3, chapter 13, "Of Experience," translated by Charles Cotton, edited by William Carew Hazlitt (1877), available online at www.gutenberg.org/files /3600/3600-h/3600-h.htm#link2HCH0106 (accessed June 30, 2014).
3. Aristotle, *Nicomachean Ethics*, book 1, section 4.

Chapter 2: In the Garden of Pleasures, with Aristotle and Epicurus

1. Aristotle, *Nicomachean Ethics*, book 7, section 13.
2. Ibid., book 1, section 4.
3. Freud, *Civilization and Its Discontents*, p. 23. See also his "Formulations Regarding the Two Principles in Mental Functioning" (1911), in *Papers on Metapsychology – Papers on Applied Psycho-Analysis*, volume 4 of *Collected Papers*, edited by Alix Strachey and Joan Riviere (London: Hogarth and Institute of Psycho-Analysis, 1924–1950), pp. 13–21.
4. Aristotle, *Nicomachean Ethics*, book 7, section 13.
5. Ibid., book 10, section 7.
6. Ibid., book 10, section 8.
7. Ibid., book 1, section 13.
8. Epicurus, fragment 469, in H. Usener, *Epicurea* (Leipzig: Teubner, 1887), p. 300.
9. Epicurus, "Letter to Menoeceus."
10. Ibid.
11. Juvenal, *Satires*, Book 10, line 356, translated by A. S. Kline,

available online at www.poetryintranslation.com/klineasjuve-nal.htm (accessed June 30, 2014).

12. Arthur Schopenhauer, *Philosophical Writings*, edited by Wolf-gang Schirmacher (London: Continuum; The German Library, 1994), p. 260.

13. I will return to this in chapter 11.

14. This question is discussed in chapter 10, below.

Chapter 3: Giving Meaning to Life

1. Seneca, *Moral Letters to Lucilius*, Loeb Classical Library, translated by Richard Mott Gummere, 3 volumes (London: W. Heinemann; Cambridge, Mass.: Harvard University Press, 1962–1967), volume 2, letter 71.

2. K. C. Berridge and M. L. Kringelbach, "Building a Neuroscience of Pleasure and Well-Being," in *Psychology of Well-Being: Theory, Research and Practice*, 2011, 1:3, available online at www.psywb.com/content/1/1/3 (accessed June 30, 2014).

Chapter 4: Voltaire and the Happy Idiot

1. Voltaire, "Story of a Good Brahmin," in *The Portable Voltaire*, edited by Ben Ray Redman (Harmondsworth: Penguin, 1977), pp. 436–38 (p. 438).

2. Comte-Sponville, *Le Bonheur désespérément*, p. 15.

Chapter 5: Does Every Human Being Wish to Be Happy?

1. Alain, *Propos sur le Bonheur*, XCII.

2. This is discussed in Saint Augustine's treatise on happiness, *De vita beata*. There is an English version, *The Happy Life*, translated and annotated by Ludwig Schopp (St. Louis: B. Herder, 1939).

3. Blaise Pascal, *Pensées*, no. 425, translated by W. S. Trotter (New York: Dutton, 1958), p. 113.

4. Matthieu Ricard, *Plaidoyer pour le Bonheur* (Paris: NiL, 1997; Pocket, 2004), p. 28.

5. Plato, *Euthydemus*, 278e, translated by Benjamin Jowett,

available online at www.gutenberg.org/files/1598/1598-h /1598-h.htm (accessed July 21, 2014).

Chapter 6: Happiness Is Not of This World: Socrates, Jesus, Kant

1. Luke 6:21. All biblical quotations are from the King James version.
2. Kant, *Groundwork for the Metaphysics of Morals*, edited and translated by Allen W. Wood (New Haven and London: Yale University Press, 2002), p. 25.
3. Ibid., p. 35.
4. Matthew 26:37–39.
5. Revelation 21:3–4.
6. Plato, *Phaedo*, 63 b–c.

Chapter 7: On the Art of Being Oneself

1. Goethe, *West-Eastern Divan*, The Book of Zuleika, part 7.
2. Gustave Flaubert, letter to Louise Colet, 13 August 1846, in *Letters of Gustave Flaubert*, pp. 61–62.
3. Goethe, *West-Eastern Divan*.

Chapter 8: Schopenhauer: Happiness Lies in Our Sensibility

1. Schopenhauer's maxims on happiness can be found in *Die Kunst, glücklich zu sein: dargestellt in fünfzig Lebensregeln*, edited by Franco Volpi (Munich: C. H. Beck, 1999).
2. Schopenhauer, *Die Kunst, glücklich zu sein*.
3. Ibid.
4. Ibid.
5. Ibid.
6. L'Essentiel, *Cerveau et Psycho*, May–July 2013, p. 14. I haven't managed to ascertain what methodology governed the investigation, and so I have to confess that I don't know how such a precise numeral assessment can be made—but I am communicating it to my readers as it stands!

Chapter 9: Does Money Make Us Happy?

1. Seneca, "On Anger," III, 30, 3, in *Moral and Political Essays*, edited and translated by John M. Cooper and J. F. Procopé (Cambridge: Cambridge University Press, 1995), p. 106.
2. Amos Tversky and Dale Griffin, "Endowments and Contracts in Judgments of Well-Being," in R. J. Zeckhauser (ed.), *Strategy and Choice* (Harvard, Mass.: MIT Press, 1991).
3. Seneca, "On Anger."
4. Marie de Vergès, "Parlons bonheur, parlons croissance," *Le Monde*, February 26, 2013.
5. Jean-Jacques Rousseau, *Dissertation on the Origin and Foundation of the Inequality of Mankind*, translated by G.D.H. Cole (New York: Dutton, 1920), available online at www.gutenberg.org/files/46333/46333-h/46333-h.htm (accessed July 21, 2014).

Chapter 10: The Emotional Brain

1. Rick Hanson, *Buddha's Brain: The Practical Neuroscience of Happiness, Love, and Wisdom* (Oakland, Calif.: New Harbinger Publications, 2009), back cover.
2. Thanks to Émile Houin and the *Petit Larousse médical* for helping me clarify some of the details in this chapter.
3. He is a former head of clinic at the Princeton Brain Bio Center and the director of the PATH medical centers in New York and Philadelphia. The information in this chapter comes from his work *Younger You: Unlock the Hidden Power of Your Brain to Look and Feel 15 Years Younger* (New York: McGraw-Hill, 2007).
4. Martin-Du Pan, *Revue médicale Suisse*, 2012, 8: pp. 627–30.
5. Jan-Emmanuel De Neve, "Functional Polymorphism (5-HTTLPR) in the Serotonin Transporter Gene Is Associated with Subjective Well-Being: Evidence from a U.S. Nationally Representative Sample," in *Journal of Human Genetics*, 56,

456-459 (June 2011); available online at www.nature.com/jhg /journal/v56/n6/full/jhg201139a.html.

Chapter 11: On the Art of Being Attentive . . . and Dreaming

1. Seneca, *Letters to Lucilius*, I, 1.
2. You can find an excellent summary of this work in the article by two psychiatrists, researchers at the hospital of La Pitié-Salpêtrière, Antoine Pelissolo and Thomas Mauras, "Le cerveau heureux," *Cerveau et Psycho*, July 2013, pp. 26–32.
3. Pelissolo and Mauras, "Le cerveau heureux."
4. One of the most popular of these works is entirely devoted to this question: see Eckhart Tolle, *The Power of Now: A Guide to Spiritual Enlightenment* (London: Hodder and Stoughton, 2005).
5. Sevim Riedinger, *Le Monde secret de l'enfant* (Paris: Carnets Nord/Éditions Montparnasse, 2013), p. 79.

Chapter 12: We Are What We Think

1. See Epictetus, *Handbook*, in *Discourses, Fragments, Handbook*, translated by Robin Hard (Oxford: Oxford University Press, "World's Classics," 2014).
2. Schopenhauer, *Die Kunst, glücklich zu sein*.
3. Ibid.
4. Ibid.
5. See his main work in 2 volumes, *Traité du désespoir et de la beatitude* (Paris: PUF, 1991).
6. Martin Seligman, *Authentic Happiness: Using the New Positive Psychology to Realize Your Potential for Lasting Fulfillment* (New York: Atria Books, 2004).

Chapter 13: The Time of a Life

1. In *Le Monde des Religions*, interview, November–December 2013.

2. P. Brickman, D. Coates, R. Janoff-Bulman, "Lottery Winners and Accident Victims: Is Happiness Relative?" *Journal of Personality and Social Psychology*, vol. 36, 1978.
3. Cédric Afsa and Vincent Marcus, "Le Bonheur attend-il le nombre des années?" France, *Social Portrait* (Paris: Insee, 2008).

Chapter 14: Can We Be Happy Without Other People?
1. Aristotle, *Nicomachean Ethics*, book 8, section 1.
2. Ibid.
3. Diogenes Laertius, *Lives of the Philosophers*, V, 20, edited by R. D. Hicks, available onnline at www.perseus.tufts.edu /hopper/text?doc=D.+L.+5.1&fromdoc=Perseus%3Atext %3A1999.01.0258 (accessed July 22, 2014).
4. Montaigne, *Essays*, book 1, chapter 27, "Of Friendship."
5. Aristotle, *Nicomachean Ethics*, book 9, section 10.
6. Montaigne, *Essays*, book 3, chapter 10, "Of Managing the Will."
7. See E. Diener, M. Seligman, "M.P.E. Very Happy People," *Psychological Science*, 2002, 13, pp. 81–84.
8. Acts, 20:35.
9. Jean-Jacques Rousseau, *The Reveries of the Solitary Walker*, translated by Charles E. Butterworth (Indianapolis, Ind.: Hackett, 1992), p. 75.
10. Matthieu Ricard, *Plaidoyer pour l'altruisme. La force de la bienveillance* (Paris: NiL, 2013), p. 777.

Chapter 15: The Contagiousness of Happiness
1. Alain, *Propos sur le Bonheur*, XCII.
2. André Gide, *Later Fruits of the Earth*, in *Fruits of the Earth*, translated by Dorothy Bussy (Harmondsworth: Penguin in association with Secker & Warburg, 1970), p. 167.
3. James H. Fowler and Nicholas A. Christakis, "Dynamic Spread

of Happiness in a Large Social Network: Longitudinal Analysis over 20 Years in the Framingham Heart Study," *British Medical Journal* December 4, 2008; 337 doi: dx.doi.org/10.1136/bmj .a2338 (published December 5, 2008).

Chapter 16: Individual Happiness and Collective Happiness

1. Spinoza, *Ethics*, translated by Edwin Curley (London: Penguin, 1996), IV, 35, corollary 2.
2. Bruckner, *L'Euphorie*, p. 45.
3. Ibid., p. 18.
4. Aristotle, *Nicomachean Ethics*, book 1, section 1.
5. I am here summarizing part of my argument in *La Guérison du Monde* (Paris: Fayard, 2012) on the three individualist revolutions.
6. Gilles Lipovetsky, *L'Ère du vide* (Paris: Gallimard, 1983).
7. See John Stuart Mill, *Utilitarianism*, chapter 2.

Chapter 17: Can the Quest for Happiness Make Us Unhappy?

1. Denis Diderot, *Éléments de physiologie*, XIII.
2. Bruckner, *L'Euphorie*, pp. 59, 86 and 93.
3. Max Weber, *The Protestant Ethic and the Spirit of Capitalism*, translated by Talcott Parsons, with an introduction by Anthony Giddens (London and New York: Routledge, 2001), p. 196, n. 79.
4. Alain Ehrenberg, *The Weariness of the Self: Diagnosing the History of Depression in the Contemporary Age*, translated by Enrico Caouette et al. (Montréal; London: McGill-Queen's University Press, 2009).
5. David Hume, "The Stoic," available online at hermetic.com /93beast.fea.st/files/section1/hume/extras/Essays,%20 Moral,%20Political,%20and%20Literary.pdf (accessed July 21, 2014).

Chapter 18: From Desire to Boredom: When Happiness Is Impossible

1. Arthur Schopenhauer, *The World as Will and Representation*, IV, 57, translated by R. B. Haldane and J. Kemp.
2. Lucretius, *De rerum natura*, book III, lines 1083–84, translated by William Ellery Leonard.
3. Immanuel Kant, *Critique of Pure Reason*, translated by Norman Kemp Smith (London: Macmillan; New York: St. Martin's Press, 1929), p. 636.
4. Schopenhauer, *The World as Will and Representation*, III, 38.
5. Ibid., IV, 57.
6. Schopenhauer, *Die Kunst, glücklich zu sein*.
7. Freud, *Civilization and Its Discontents*, p. 23.

Chapter 19: The Smile of the Buddha and Epictetus

1. Epictetus, *Handbook*, p. 288.
2. Tilopa was a Buddhist sage of the ninth century.
3. Epictetus, p. 292.
4. Ibid., p. 289.
5. Ibid., pp. 289–90.
6. Readers who would like to go more deeply into this question should consult the major work by Jean-Christophe Kolm, *Le Bonheur-liberté, bouddhisme profound et modernité* (Paris: PUF, 1982).
7. Quoted in Jean-François Revel, *Histoire de la philosophie occidentale* (Paris: NiL, 1994), p. 212; the text here quotes the translation of the *Meditations* of Marcus Aurelius by George Long, available online at classics.mit.edu/Antoninus/meditations .mb.txt (accessed July 22, 2014).

Chapter 20: The Laughter of Montaigne and Chuang Tzu

1. Montaigne, *Essays*, book 3, chapter 13, "Of Experience."

2. *Complete Works of Chuang Tzu*, translated by Burton Watson (New York: Columbia University Press, 1968), pp. 187–88.

3. Montaigne, *Essays*, book 3, chapter 13, "Of Experience."

4. Cicero says "For the whole life of a philosopher is [...] a meditation on death," in *Tusculan Disputations*, translated by C. D. Yonge (New York: Harper & Brothers, 1877), p. 41, available online at www.gutenberg.org/files/14988/14988-h /14988-h.htm (accessed July 21, 2014).

5. Montaigne, *Essays*, book 3, chapter 9, "Of Vanity."

6. Ibid., book 2, chapter 12, "Apology for Raimond Sebond."

7. Ibid.

8. Marcel Conche, *Montaigne ou la conscience heureuse* (Paris: PUF, 2002), p. 63.

9. Montaigne, *Essays*, book 1, chapter 37, "That We Laugh and Cry for the Same Thing."

10. Ibid., book 2, chapter 12, "Apology for Raimond Sebond."

11. Ibid., book 1, chapter 30, "Of Cannibals."

12. Ibid., book 1, chapter 24, "Of Pedantry."

13. Ibid., book 3, chapter 9, "Of Vanity."

14. Ibid., book 3, chapter 13, "Of Experience."

15. Ibid., book 1, chapter 40, "That the Relish of Good and Evil Depends in Great Measure upon the Opinion we Have of Them."

16. Ibid., book 3, chapter 13, "Of Experience."

17. Specialists transcribe these names more rigorously as Laozi and Zhuangzi, but I prefer here to use the old transcription (Lao Tzu and Chuang Tzu) as it is better known to the general public.

18. *Complete Works of Chuang Tzu*, pp. 187–88.

19. Lao Tzu, *Tao Te Ching*, translated by John C. H. Wu, chapter 14, available online at terebess.hu/english/tao/wu.html (accessed July 20, 2014).

20. *Complete Works of Chuang Tzu*.

21. Lao Tzu, *Tao Te Ching*, chapter 29.

22. Ibid., chapter 37.

23. *Complete Works of Chuang Tzu*, p. 205.
24. Antoine Compagnon, *Un été avec Montaigne* (Paris: France Inter/éditions des Équateurs, coll. "Parallèles," 2013), p. 20.
25. Lao Tzu, *Tao Te Ching*, chapter 78.
26. Ibid., chapter 28.
27. *Complete Works of Chuang Tzu*, pp. 191–92.
28. Ibid., p. 29.
29. Conche, *Montaigne*, pp. 88–89.

Chapter 21: The Joy of Spinoza and Ma Anandamayi

1. Spinoza, *Ethics*, III, 2.
2. Quoted in Antonio Damasio, *Looking for Spinoza: Joy, Sorrow and the Feeling Brain* (London: Vintage, 2004).p. 253.
3. Revel, *Histoire de la philosophie occidentale*, p. 404.
4. Spinoza, *Ethics*, part IV, Preface.
5. Ibid., part III, Preface.
6. Ibid., III, 2, scholium.
7. Ibid., III, prop. 6.
8. Damasio, *Looking for Spinoza*, p. 36.
9. Spinoza, *Ethics*, III, 13, scholium.
10. Ibid., IV, 8, demonstration.
11. Spinoza, letter 19 to Blyenbergh.
12. Gilles Deleuze, *Spinoza. Practical Philosophy*, translated by Robert Hurley (San Francisco, CA: City Lights Books, 1988).
13. Spinoza, *Ethics*, IV, 35, corollary 2.
14. Ibid., IV, 18, demonstration. "This is where the originality and modernity of Spinozism reside," notes Robert Misrahi, one of the most enlightening exegetes of Spinoza. Misrahi has attempted to investigate in depth the notions of desire and liberty as seen from the viewpoint of modern thought (*Le Bonheur*, p. 32), see also his *100 mots sur l'Éthique de Spinoza* (Paris: Les Empêcheurs de tourner en rond, 2005).
15. Spinoza, *Ethics*, III, 9, scholium.

16. Ibid., III, 39, scholium.
17. Ibid., IV, proposition 7.
18. Ibid., IV, Preface and 4, demonstration.
19. Spinoza, *Tractatus theologico-politicus*, IV, 4, translated by Samuel Shirley (Leiden: Brill, 1991).
20. Spinoza, *Ethics*, V, 42, scholium.
21. Ibid., I, 15, proposition.
22. "Chandogya Upanishad," in *The Upanishads*, translated by Valerie J. Roebuck (New Delhi; London: Penguin Books, 2000), p. 206.
23. Spinoza, *Ethics*, V, 23, scholium.
24. Bruno Giuliani, *Le Bonheur avec Spinoza* (Paris: Éditions Almora, 2011). In this book, the author puts forward a very bold rewriting of the *Ethics* adapted to today's world. His text is often very far removed from Spinoza's, even if he always stays faithful to his spirit.
25. See Alexander Lipsky, *Life and teaching of Śrī Ānandamayī Mā* (Delhi: Motilal Banarsidass, 1979).
26. See the collection of unpublished texts in Ma Andamayi, *Retrouver la joie*, preface by Arnaud Desjardins (Paris: Le Relié, 2010), p. 11.
27. See www.einsteinandreligion.com/spinoza.html.
28. *Ethics*, in *Ethics, Treatise on The Emendation of the Intellect, and Selected Letters*, translated by Samuel Shirley, edited and introduced by Seymour Feldman (Indianapolis, Indiana: Hackett Publishing Company, 1992), V, proposition 42, scholium.

Epilogue

1. In *Le Monde des Religions*, interview, November–December 2013.
2. Etty Hillesum: *An Interrupted Life: The Diaries and Letters of Etty Hillesum, 1941–43*, with a preface by Eva Hoffman;

and introduction by Jan G. Gaarlandt; translated by Arnold J. Pomerans (London: Persephone, 1999), June 29, 1942 (p. 150).

3. Ibid., pp. 63 and 70.
4. Bruckner, *L'Euphorie*, p. 255.
5. Misrahi, *Le Bonheur*, p. 56.

Bibliography

Classics (in chronological order)
Buddha, *Sermons*
Lao Tzu, *Tao Te Ching*
Chuang Tzu, *The Book of Chuang Tzu*
Plato, *Apology*
Aristotle, *Nicomachean Ethics*
Epicurus, *Letter to Menoeceus and Other Works*
Lucretius, *De rerum natura*
Epictetus, *Handbook and Other Works*
Seneca, *Letters to Lucilius*
Marcus Aurelius, *Meditations*
Montaigne, *Essays*
Pascal, *Pensées*
Spinoza, *Ethics*
Immanuel Kant, *Groundwork for the Metaphysics of Morals*
Arthur Schopenhauer, *The World as Will and Representation*
Sigmund Freud, *Civilization and Its Discontents*
Alain, *Propos sur le bonheur*
Etty Hillesum, *Interrupted Life*
Ma Anandamayi, *Life and Teaching*

Select Bibliography

Eric Braverman, *Younger Brain, Sharper Mind* (Emmaus, PA: Rodale Press, 2013).

Pascal Bruckner, *L'Euphorie perpétuelle* (Paris: Grasset, 2000; Le Livre de Poche, 2002).

Antoine Companon, *Un été avec Montaigne* (Paris: France Inter/Éditions des Équateurs, coll. "Parallèles," 2013).

André Comte-Sponville, *Le Traité du désespoir et de la beatitude* (Paris: PUF, 1984); *Le Bonheur désespérément* (Paris: Pleins feux, 2000; Librio, 2009).

Marcel Conche, *Montaigne ou la conscience heureuse* (Paris: PUF, 2002).

Antonio Damasio, *Looking for Spinoza: Joy, Sorrow and the Feeling Brain* (London: Vintage, 2004).

Gilles Deleuze, *Spinoza, Practical Philosophy*, translated by Robert Hurley (San Francisco, CA: City Lights Books, 1988).

Alain Ehrenberg, *The Weariness of the Self: Diagnosing the History of Depression in the Contemporary Age*, translated by Enrico Caouette et al. (Montréal; London: McGill-Queen's University Press, 2009).

Luc Ferry, *Qu'est-ce qu'une vie réussie?* (Paris: Grasset, 2002).

Bruno Giuliani, *Le Bonheur avec Spinoza* (Paris: Almora, 2011).

Pierre Hadot, *Philosophy as a Way of Life: Spiritual Exercises from Socrates to Foucault*, edited with an introduction by Arnold I. Davidson, translated by Michael Chase (Oxford: Blackwell, 1995).

Rick Hanson, *Buddha's Brain: The Practical Neuroscience of Happiness, Love, and Wisdom* (Oakland, CA: New Harbinger Publications, 2009).

Alexandre Jollien, *Petit traité de l'abandon* (Paris: Seuil, 2012).

Serge-Christophe Kolm, *Le bonheur-liberté, bouddhisme profond et modernité* (Paris: PUF, revised edition, 1994).

Robert Misrahi, *100 mots sur l'*Éthique de Spinoza (Paris: Les empêcheurs de tourner en rond, 2005); *Spinoza, une philosophie de la joie* (Paris: Entrelacs, 2005); *Le Bonheur, essai sur la joie* (Paris: Cécile Defaut, 2011).

Michel Onfray, *La Puissance d'exister* (Paris: Grasset, 2006).

Jean-François Revel, *Histoire de la philosophie occidentale* (Paris: NiL, 1994).

Matthieu Ricard, *Happiness: A Guide to Developing Life's Most Important Skill* (London: Atlantic Books; new edition, 2007).

Martin Seligman, *Learned Optimism* (New York; London: Pocket Books, 1998); *Authentic Happiness: Using the New Positive Psychology to Realize Your Potential for Lasting Fulfillment* (New York: Atria Books, 2004).